Investing in Real Prop Beginners

Buy Low and Rent High

By

George Stallion

The trademarks that are used are without any consent, and the publication of the trademark is without permission or backing by the trademark owner. All trademarks and brands within this book are for clarifying purposes only and are owned by the owners themselves, not affiliated with this document.

Table of contents

Introduction

The goal of the investment is to put resources into assets so that one expands his profits and limits the chances of risks. The investor may have different destinations, and one needs to accomplish a proper equilibrium among them. Any single target ought not to be given unnecessary significance at the expense of the others. The investment goals of investors might be to get steady current returns, to seek raise in the value of the venture and to enjoy tax cover by gaining in tax exemption ventures. The real investment includes that in land and buildings, gold and silver.

Real estate consists of the buying, possession, the execution, and rental as well as selling of land and buildings for gains. Real property investment is a large business, and, whenever done appropriately, could immediately turn out to be exceptionally rewarding. One factor that differentiates real investing from financial one is the liquidity. Liquidity indicates the convertibility of a resource in to cash rapidly, advantageously, and at little trade cost. Real resources are less liquid than financial resources generally in light of non-existence of organized business sectors and exchanging framework. Stock markets would provide almost the same for financial speculations. Since real investment includes trade of genuine property, when the property is transferred, the danger of vulnerability is least.

Notwithstanding, the party at risk in financial investment to give returns might or might not be able to meet their obligation always. Regardless of whether it does, it probably would not be on a fixed schedule. Thus, vulnerability is there in financial ventures. Putting resources into rental property effectively is dependent upon a few variables.

For this situation, the sum is probably equivalent to all the parts, as all requirements need to fit in for a rental property venture to remunerate investors. Some rental property speculators permit themselves to be stuck by overthinking and never complete the deals.

Consequently, they wind up, paying an overabundance significantly than needed. There is no general definition that exists to characterize a "great" rental property. Doling out quite an abstract moniker to a resource is practically subjective, however saying this does not imply that there are not various signs to search for. While by all account, not the only indications of a decent rental property, the following attributes are practically general in their existence: Cash Flow and Growth Potential, Location, Property Condition, Property Value, Property Management and Market Trends.

One expected benefit of pooling money into a rental is that it can produce two types of returns. It could give the increase as time goes on if the property estimation increases over the long run and because of upgrades made by the proprietor, and as the proprietor builds value in the property by settling the mortgage. Second, the proprietor additionally could understand a progressing return as sure income on the venture — acquired by leasing the property out to inhabitants for regularly scheduled instalments that surpass the proprietor's general monthly costs to keep up the property. This book is an ultimate guide for new investors to purchase the real property on low prices and rent it out on higher prices, to make the desirable gains doing so. The strategies might prove to be helpful, depending upon the location of real estate and mindsets of the investors regarding their next move.

Chapter 1: Real Estate - An Introduction

Among all accessible venture alternatives, real property is that with which purchasers would, generally, get sincerely associated with. Consequently, individuals legitimize their enthusiastic choices with the assistance of numerous myths about investments in real properties.

In case, one does not want to get ensnared in various areas of the real estate investments and settle on financially steady choices; fundamentally, all the myths about real estate be perceived and excused. A well-known myth perceived by various advocates and land sales representatives of real property investment is that the land is scant. There is just a restricted measure of land on the planet. This, combined with the fact that the world's population is expanding concludes that the land costs of the world will keep on rising unendingly since there will consistently be a deficiency of land.

Nonetheless, a glance at the numbers will clarify that this is not the situation. Initially, the facts demonstrate that there is a restricted measure of land on the planet. Be that as it may, innovative improvement is making it conceivable to utilize this land. Studies have been carried out, and their decisions express that regardless of whether the number of inhabitants on the planet was to rise four creases, there would, in any case, be a bountiful area of land for an entire population to endure and flourish.

Besides, researches have likewise been led which express that the planet's population would stabilize. This implies that the populace development time has reached its pinnacle and now the inhabitants' statistics would be steady. Henceforth, the "land is scant and consequently valuable" rationale is only the proliferation of a myth.

Another myth is that land prices always go up in value. This reasoning is predominant, largely, in developing economies which have experienced a remarkable rise in real estate area in the past decade. The cost of land in these economies has gone up multiple times in the previous twenty years. Thus, individuals in these nations have come to accept that the cost of land consistently rises; that is, the real properties investments consistently go up in worth. This is a long way from actuality. If one ponders on developed economies such as Japan and the United States, one could discover instances of land crashes where costs have dropped to the tune of 40% to 50%. In Japan, the costs have gone down and have kept on remaining there for pretty much the most recent decade.

Subsequently, indeed, "land costs consistently appreciate in worth" is a mythical assertion. Land prices are based on numerous factors; one such element is the economic prosperity. Some investors in real estate assume that past performance predicts future performance.

There is an inclination among hopeful real property speculators to extrapolate the trends which existed in property markets before and create a very thoughtless future situation. Notwithstanding, one requires to comprehend that the world has gone through an essential move in the most recent decade. Business game plans such as outsourcing, cross border ventures and free trade by multinational firms had created a shock wave in the arising economies. The future does not hold any such transformation in its offing. On the off chance that no sudden financial transformation in a general sense changes the world's economic perspective, it is unlikely that the demonstration of previous few years is rehashed in later years. Speculators wagering on an encore are in for a discourteous stun.

There is another myth that real estate investments could be flipped easily. This is anything but a common misconception. Nonetheless, before the subprime emergency broke out in the United States, cases of independent land merchants who owed their fortunes solely to buying and selling the land on borrowed cash were usual.

Such tycoons spread the morality of flipping, that is, purchasing and selling land a few times in a brief period. The thought was to book the benefit emerging from the value differential and changing over it into money.

Notwithstanding, what those merchants neglected to refer to was the tremendous amount of exchange expenses that were associated with any land exchange worldwide. Along these lines, the more properties one flips, the higher exchange costs they incur. These exchange costs add up to anyplace between 2% to 5% of the cost of the property being referred to.

Aside from the exchange costs, finding a willing purchaser and arranging a deal is a dull and tedious cycle. Flipping properties thus causes enormous seepage of time, same as assets, and subsequently should be evaded quite far.

There is a common belief in real estate markets that buying is better than renting. Property buyers worldwide have an enthusiastic affiliation with the real estate they purchase. From conventional occasions, purchasing land has been considered the "grown-up" activity for an individual. This choice has no monetary support and is found in the notion that possessing a property by any means makes one financially secure.

In any case, if we consider the monetary perspectives, such a notion is false. There are a few circumstances when purchasing is unmistakably the better activity, though there are different circumstances where leasing is the ideal alternative. The ideal activity accordingly relies upon a case-to-case premise.

1.1 What is Real Estate?

Real estate implies the land along with any lasting improvements attached to the land, regardless of whether human-made or natural—including trees, water, minerals, fences, homes, structures and scaffolds. Real estate is a type of real property. It contrasts from individual property that includes things not forever connected to the land, such as, vehicles, boats, furniture, gems, and farm hardware.

A real estate is a group of "real property" that incorporates land and anything for all time joined to it, regardless of whether natural or human-made. There are five principal classifications of land: commercial, residential, raw land, industrial and the one for a particular use.

You could put resources into real estate straightforwardly by buying a home, rental property or other property, or by implication through a Real Estate Venture Trust (REIT). Individuals regularly utilize the terms real estate, land, and real property conversely, however, there are some inconspicuous differences. Land refers to the soil's surface below the center point of the earth and ascending to the airspace upwards, including the minerals, trees and water. Real estate includes the land, along with any perpetual human-made increments, for instance, different structures and houses. Whereas, one of the two principal arrangements of real property incorporates the interests, rights and benefits inalienable in the proprietorship of real estate.

Extensively, the real estate incorporates the actual surface of the land, what lies above and beneath it, what is forever joined to it, in addition to all the privileges of proprietorship— including the option to have, sell, rent, and use the land. Real property should not be mistaken for personal property, which envelops all property that does not fit the meaning of real property.

The essential trait of personal property is that it is versatile. Examples are boats, vehicles, garments, furniture and cell phones.

Physical Features of Real Estate

The land has three physical attributes that separate it from different resources in the economy:

1. It is immobile. While a few pieces of land are removable and the topography could be modified, the geographic area of any part of the land can never be changed.

2. The land is indestructible. The land is sturdy and indestructible (lasting).

3. The land has its uniqueness. No two parts of land could be equivalent. Even though they may share likenesses, each piece varies geographically.

Economic Features of Real Estate

Land likewise has some specific economic aspects that impact its incentive as a venture:

- **Shortage:** While the land is not viewed as rare, the aggregate supply is fixed.

- **Improvements:** Any increases or changes to the land or building that influences the property's estimated value is called an improvement. Upgrades of a private sort, (for example, homes and fences) are alluded to as enhancements for the land. Upgrades of a public sort (e.g., walkways and sewer frameworks) are also the enhancements to the land.

- **Lastingness of Investment:** Once the land is improved, the complete labor and capital used to assemble the improvement denote sizable fixed speculation. Even though a building could be bulldozed, enhancements such as drainage, power, water, and sewer frameworks will, in general, be perpetual because they cannot be removed (or supplanted) economically.

- **Area or territory inclination:** Area alludes to individuals' decisions and tastes concerning a given zone, given components like accommodation, notoriety, and history. The area is one of the main economic aspects of the land.

Facts about Real Property

Real property, sometimes alluded to as "real estate," "immovable property," or "realty" is made out of any assigned segment of land and anything permanently put onto or under it. The components on or under the land could incorporate natural assets and additionally man-made structures. In the legitimate sense, claiming real property includes the heap of rights shifted from merchant to purchaser upon the offer of a property. These rights regularly direct the utilization, transfer, as well as sale of real properties. These real estate entitlements incorporate the privilege of ownership, control, disposition, exclusion, and enjoyment.

Sorts of Estates Interlinked with Real Property

Various sorts of estates, which are perceived by law, further characterize the real estate rights related to property proprietorship. The sort of domain relies upon the conditions of the deed, rent, will, land grant, or potentially bill of an offer through which the inheritance was gotten.

Fee Simple Possession- likewise called "fee simple absolute," is the most well-known sort of freehold proprietorship on real property. This is the most noteworthy conceivable sort of proprietorship interest that a real property holder could have. The individuals who own properties under this kind of possession reserve the option to sell the house, leave it to their recipients, or make changes, regardless of whether they owe an amount on their mortgage.

These rights are limited by government forces of necessary buy, escheat, tax collection and police power.

Life Estate — this possession implies the proprietor may just claim and utilize the elaborate properties during their lifetime and may not leave the property to another person. Proprietors of life estates are classified as "life occupants." The deed illuminates what befalls the property after the existence inhabitant dies.

Future Interest — such proprietorship has a place with the individuals who will claim properties later on. The privileges of proprietors of future interest exclude the use, possession and enjoyment regarding the elaborate properties in the present. Current holders of properties may make a term of a deed or a permanent trust that permits the future interest proprietor to acquire the elaborate properties when the current proprietor passes away.

Unforeseen or Contingent Interest — in unexpected interest, the elaborate properties are not passed to the assigned inheritors except if at least one or more states of the current proprietor are satisfied. On the off chance that these conditions are not met, the properties are passed to somebody else.

Lienholder — otherwise called "lienors," are holders of a judgment lien, mortgage, deed of trust, as well as technician's lien on real estate. Lienholders have a possession interest in the included real properties.

Real Property versus Personal Property

Current law makes a good differentiation between real property (instances of real property incorporate land and anything fastened to it) and personal property (attire, furniture, cash). Property that cannot be isolated based on what is viewed as real property would be viewed as real property.

Real Property versus Real Estate

As the real property is land and anything that is undaunted upon it, there could be a hazy situation with regards to real estate. The meaning of real estate is "property in structures and land," which makes it real property. Nonetheless, legitimate issues could emerge when a landowner determines that an area of real property does not have any significant bearing to the deal price of real estate or the other way around. The essential qualification comes down to the heap of rights, referenced previously. Real property comprises of both physical articles and customary law rights, while real estate comprises just of psychical items. Each state has various laws concerning what is real property and how to deal with its sale; generally, real property is not dependent upon government law.

Real Property Law

Explicit real property laws overseeing real property and the estates they incorporate are declared by the states and, generally, not dependent upon government law. These regulations apply to land, just as anything that is fixed to the land, for example, structures or joined equipment. In certain states, whatever lies under a plot of land is essential for that real property. In different states whatever lies underneath, or goes through, a property might be dependent upon various laws, with discrete possession. This could incorporate valuable gems, metals, ore and even water.

To be genuine, an assertion to any real property must be joined by a clear and lawful property depiction. Such a portrayal, for the most part, utilizes characteristic or artificial limits, for example, waterways, seacoasts, streams, lakeshores, the peaks of ridges, parkways, or purpose-constructed markers, for example, surveyor's posts, fences, cairns, and official government surveying marks.

1.2 Types of Real Estates

Real property comes in a wide range of types and can profit the investors of real estate on numerous unique and alternate views in their speculations. The real estate speculators may concentrate on multifamily homes in the residential class. Or on the other hand, they might have their specialty in office spaces in the commercial class. They could even put resources into farms, stores, manufacturing plants, office space. The fact is, there are numerous kinds of real property to construct your real estate contributing business from.

Agricultural

Agriculture includes utilizing the land to give crops, raise animals and plants (trees, plantations). These kinds of ventures may offer a different portfolio that incorporates a significant number of similar advantages of real estate speculations. The investors may purchase, sell, and rent a farming property. The speculators may likewise put resources into the genuine agricultural business itself, for example, purchasing a homestead or farm that produces beef cattle, while at the same time having the rancher or farmer deal with the activity.

Sorts of Agricultural Property

Farms

A farm is a region of land that is principally given to agricultural utilizations, creating plants, food and raising animals.

Ranches

A ranch is like a farm and can be equivalent. Nonetheless, the basic contrast is that a farm produces food and different yields and a ranch effectively raises grazing animals, for example, cows and sheep.

Forest Area

Forest area or timberland is real property that is covered with backwoods and is reasonable for wood. There are a few different ways that a speculator could put resources into the forest area, for example, Exchange Traded Funds or ETFs, lumber, and REITs or Real Estate Investment Trusts that contain forest area related items. Furthermore, the speculator could buy the land-related with the lumber and sell the wood.

Orchards

It is a real property that contains planted fruit trees, for example, oranges, apples, grapes.

Residential

Another sort of real property incorporates homes. These properties in the private classification, explicitly address multifamily lodging and single-family lodging in metropolitan, rural and rustic territories. Individuals are headed to buy a real property through the residential class, in that, many take a stab at homeownership.

Home Ownership

Homeownership, for many investors, brings monetary stability, and many accept that it is a resource that incorporates drawn-out speculation. Nonetheless, a house is just a resource on the off chance that it places cash in your pocket, and it is an obligation when everything it does is to remove cash from your pocket. As such, your home is not a resource; it is an obligation, except if, you have a satisfactory income from the real property.

However, it does not forestall the way that numerous individuals want and long for homeownership in any event, even when it is an obligation. There are advantages and weaknesses of homeownership, yet whatever the decision you make, be sure that if any obligation is taken out, figure out how the home loan industry functions and study how you can utilize a HELOC (Home Equity Line of Credit) to take care of the home quicker, in this manner, sparing thousands and more in interest with the help of velocity banking.

Sorts of Residential Property

Single-family Homes

Single-family homes may incorporate attached or detached homes, for example, townhouses. Also, single-family homes might be the most broadly utilized and well-known lodging types for real property.

High Rises

High rises or multifamily units permit many swarmed territories to get lodging for individuals. These structures are generally situated in metropolitan regions and suburban zones. It is uncommon to see anything similar to a high rise in a rural territory. These structures may likewise acquire security, laundromat, clubhouse, pool, parking, wellness club, and now and again, a golf club. Numerous investors prefer the multifamily units in light of its constraints on risks, absence of competition, and easy management. In any case, a larger degree of capital is typically required for these kinds of real property ventures.

Condominium

The condominium is equivalent to a high rise, besides regarding proprietorship. Where a high rise is claimed by one business or proprietor, a condominium might be possessed exclusively.

These townhouses will have a Home Ownership Association or the board that will be answerable for the overall upkeep of the structure. The condos are a lot of like high rises, in that, they share normal components, for example, lifts, security framework, tennis court, pool, and different conveniences.

Cooperatives

A cooperative is one of a different sort of homeownership, in that, when a speculator buys into a property, you become an investor in an organization who possesses the real property. Every investor is qualified for possessing one lodging unit for each investor arrangement. It is a pooling of cooperative individuals that picks up its advantages in the purchasing power by bringing down the expense of member's upkeep and services.

Manufactured Housing

Manufactured homes or plant-assembled homes are constructed totally from the production lines, conveyed to the site and then installed. In the United States, these homes are worked under the oversight and managed by the US Branch of Housing and Urban Development (HUD). Preceding June 15, 1976, these kinds of homes were known as mobile houses. These homes could be moderately cheaper because of their assembly-line type development from their manufacturing plants and the present-day styles with space are making these kinds of homes more alluring to purchasers.

Planned Unit Developments (PUDs)

A PUD, additionally called master-planned community is a building improvement that may comprise of the whole habitation, or it might likewise be viable in its improvement with land uses, for example, amusement, business focuses, or industrial parks. PUDs are arranged to utilize special-zoning statutes. Licenses permit developments to augment the space by diminishing part sizes or road areas.

In many PUDs, proprietors have full responsibility for structures and homes, subsequently, making them sole duty for upkeep, in any case, the roads, pedestrian walkways, sidewalks and parks would be appointed to the association of homeowners. Further, PUD may incorporate a small expansion or include a whole arranged-out city.

Converted-Use Properties

These properties, also called conversion properties, are structures that are changed over into residential use. As such, the structures could be schools, temples, warehouses and different kinds of buildings that are remodeled into residential properties. Usually, it is economically and financially sound to remodel the framework of the building as opposed to knocking it down. For example, a warehouse might be revamped into a school, or it could be redesigned into a shopping center (business property).

Commercial Real Estate

Commercial property is another kind of real property. Such property incorporates the property that contains business pursuits, for example, office spaces, shopping plazas, malls, stores, and amusement facilities. Additionally, inns, hotels, as well as parking slots, are different kinds of commercial property.

Kinds of Commercial Property

Business Property

Business property may incorporate any real property that is possessed by a business element. All the more significantly, the business property can allude to the activity and location of a genuine business. For example, a technician shop that has a carport is viewed as business property.

Office Space

Office space is a property that has a zone that permits business action to happen. It could include organizations that rent out office spaces to independent ventures or to individuals who do not have to lease office spaces on a full-time responsibility. They usually offer rents dependent on use and offer a few zones of office space, for example, meeting rooms.

Shopping Malls

Shopping malls are the real property that generally manages retail. Numerous speculators search out Real Estate Investment Trusts that are shopping centres ventures.

Stores

The retail industry is another speculation zone that could grow a speculators portfolio.

Theatres

Amusement, for example, theatres and film edifices are parts of real commercial property. This is another elective speculation that could benefit the investors.

Hotels

Hotels are worthwhile real property and numerous real estate speculators, when they grow their estate portfolio, at last, put resources into the hotel business.

Parking Lots

Another option and frequently ignored sort of real property are parking areas. With Artificial Intelligence (AI) and updated technologies (for example, applications), these parking garages and services could rapidly go to autopilot, which requires limited administration.

Industrial Estates

Industrial is another kind of real property that includes buildings, for example, power plants, warehouses and factories. For some speculators, the industrial zone is the least focused and discussed real property to put resources into. However, putting resources into modern land ought not to be neglected by investors.

Kinds of Industrial Property

Warehouses

A warehouse is a prerequisite that is utilized to store merchandise and assets. However, these facilities do not just store the merchandise and leave them there for an extended period; numerous warehouses are dynamic, in that, wholesalers, exporters and importers utilize these stockrooms to keep items and products moving to their clients. An investor should observe the likely potential outcomes of warehouse speculations.

Factories

The manufacturing plant can likewise be known as a factory and comprises of equipment, machinery and buildings where products are made in a complex, orderly activity. On a side note, manufacturing plants began during the industrial revolution when numerous products could not catch up with the demand and supply from small-scale workshops. In any case, manufacturing plants are another ignored venture. In some cases, the most overlooked investments might prove to be the greatest ones.

Power Plants

Power stations or power plants produce electricity and electric power. The development has permitted us to make some interesting and possibly groundbreaking ventures.

Mixed-Use

Mixed-used property is a kind of real property that has multiple utilizations for that resource. That is, for example, residential and commercial zones inside the same property.

Special Purpose

Special purpose property is a sort of real property that is normally publicly held, for example, religious spots, libraries, schools, government buildings, graveyards, and parks.

1.3 All about Rental Property

Putting resources into rental properties is an extraordinary beginning stage for real estate speculators. Rental properties could generate income and create an incentive from appreciation. Speculators additionally get tax motives and exclusions from possessing real estates. While it tends to be a rewarding technique for real property investments, there is a great deal to know before putting resources into rental properties. A rental property means a commercial or residential property that is rented or leased to an inhabitant throughout a set timeframe. Similar to the vacation rentals, there are short-term rentals, as well as long-term, similar to those leased under one-to-three-year.

Residential Rental Property

Such property alludes to homes that are bought by an investor and possessed by inhabitants on any kind of rental contract or a lease agreement. Residential property is the one that is utilized explicitly for living for the families or individuals; it might incorporate independent single-family homes to huge, multi-unit high rises.

How Residential Rental Property Operates?

A residential rental property may include apartments, single-family homes, condominium, duplexes and other such structures. The difference between a residential rental property and commercial properties is that in the commercial zone tenant would commonly be a corporate identity as opposed to an individual or family-just as lodgings and inns where an occupant does not live in the property over long-term.

Residential rental investment property could be alluring speculation. In contrast to stocks, fates, and other monetary ventures, numerous individuals have firsthand involvement in both the rental market as occupants and the real residential ventures as house-owners. This knowledge of the cycle and the venture makes residential rental properties more investor-friendly than other speculations. On top of the commonality factor, residential rental investments could offer month to month income, leverage on the borrowed amount, long-term value appreciation, along with the previously mentioned tax benefits on the inflow the speculation produces.

Possessing a residential rental property could grant tax leverages that other, more aberrant real estate ventures including Real Estate Investment Trust (REIT) do not present to the holder. Direct responsibility for residential rental property additionally accompanies the duty to go about as a landowner or involve a property management organization alongside the risks from un-occupied units to the tenant disputes.

Residential Rental Property Risks

There are some relating disadvantages to residential rental investment.

The major one is that such property is not largely a liquid venture. Income and appreciation are huge, yet on the off chances that a property quits conveying one or both because of mismanagement or economic situations, avoiding losses and getting away from it may be troublesome. To sell a declining rental property, you need to discover a purchaser to get an incentive in the speculation that you at this point do not see or which essentially is not there.

There are likewise extensive headaches that accompany going about as a landowner, albeit indulging in a property management organization could help, and that expense devours further into the net margin of the speculation. At last, there is a danger made by altering tax codes. The tax management of residential rental property could change, eradicating some of the charms of the speculation.

Tax Handling of Residential Rental Property

In some nations, residential rental property is considered to be the one that generates over 80% of its income from the dwelling units. The residential rental property utilizes the 27.5-year Modified Accelerated Cost Recovery System (MACRS) plan regarding depreciation. Inflows from residential rental property are treated as a passive revenue, so there are rules for how losses are dealt with, dependent on the dynamic interest of the proprietor. The relevant laws are updated when the provisions alter.

Commercial Rental Property

Commercial property is an estate that is utilized for business exercises. Business property typically alludes to structures that house organizations, however, can likewise allude to land used to produce a benefit, along with huge residential rental properties. The assignment of a property as a commercial property has inferences for how it is financed, taxed, and how various laws are applied to it.

Bifurcating Commercial Rental Property

Rental Commercial property incorporates shopping centres, supermarkets, workplaces, modern homes, manufacturing outlets and others. The presentation of commercial property — including deal prices, latest building rates, and inhabitance rates — is frequently utilized as a measure for business activity in a certain district or economy. For instance, the Residential Commercial Property Price Indices measure the value changes in a commercial estate in the United States.

Commercial versus Residential Property Investment

Commercial property has customarily been viewed as sound speculation. Initial venture costs for the structure and expenses related to customization for occupants are higher than those in residential real estate. Nevertheless, returns could be higher, and some basic complexities that accompany residential tenants resolve when coping with clear leases and companies.

Commercial property speculators could likewise use the triple net rent, whereby costs, for example, land charges, building insurance and upkeep are borne by the organization renting the premises. This favorable position is not accessible to residential estate investors.

Notwithstanding favorable renting terms, the commercial property would, in general profit by more clear pricing estimates. A residential property speculator must consider various aspects, including the enthusiastic allure of a property to planned occupants. Comparatively, a commercial property speculator could depend on income statement showing the valuation of present leases, which could then be contrasted against the capitalization pace of other commercial property in the territory.

Commercial Property Investment through REITS

REITs are an ideal alternative on the off chance that you need to put resources into the commercial property; however, do not have the capital or want to purchase an entire building. REITs work like shared funds, such that they pool venture dollars to purchase resources. Each offer in a REIT indicates an organization's hidden resources. Purchasing securities in a REIT that has some expertise in commercial property introduces you to such area without expecting you to purchase a building individually.

Advantages of Rental Property Investment

1. Continuous Income

Real estate speculators regularly procure 8% to 12% yields on the resources they put into investment properties starting from the very first day. At the point when you purchase a turnkey property through Roofstock, it either accompanies a paying occupant effectively settled up, or the property is in lease-prepared condition for investors to fill right away. Furthermore, in contrast to a bond's coupon, rental inflows ascend over the long-run, assisting with securing you against the moderate inflation decay.

2. Inflation Protection

In addition to the fact that rents rise with inflation, they also add to inflation. With every passing year, property owners could raise rents to stay up with or even outperform inflation. It merits whatever individuals are content to pay. This makes rental properties brilliant support against inflation.

What is more, rental speculators come out farther ahead than simply securing against inflation deficits. When you leverage others' resources, you secure your borrowing costs in the present dollars — which would, in general, lose an incentive over the long run. So even as your income mixes with an extra 2% to 6% every year, your home loan costs remain fixed.

3. Leveraging Other's Money

Speculators could regularly purchase rental properties with simply 15% to 25% of their cash, and borrow others' cash to cover the remainder of the expense. You will purchase and keep the resource. However, you might not need to pay for it completely all alone.

It is an exemplary instance of good obligation − a liability that renders you better-off as opposed to deficient. On the off chance that you acquire $80,000 to purchase a $100,000 rental property, you bring in $1,500 in normal money stream every year, at that point, you become better-off for having obtained such a debt. Then, your inhabitants pay down that obligation for you. At last, they take care of it totally, and afterwards, your income truly expands.

4. Predicted Returns

While purchasing a stock, you trust in the best dependent on past returns, and on your examination and feelings about the organization's capability to develop. Yet, no one could tell what returns it will create for you. With rental properties, you could conjecture your income and pay yield with accuracy. You realize the buying price, the market lease rate, and you could precisely appraise all costs.

5. Appreciation

The possible long-term appreciation of rental properties is less anticipated yet significant. By and large, real estate fills in an incentive over the long haul. Appreciation assists rental speculators with growing their net value over the long-run, even as their mortgage balance gradually declines. You generate inflow on rental money stream. You bring in cash on the appreciation. Furthermore, with both, you pay less in tax charges than on various other ventures.

6. Tax Benefits

Rental properties accompany enticing tax cuts that you could avail regardless of whether you take the standard discounting instead of itemizing. Real estate speculators could deduct each possible cost, including property administration expenses, mortgage interest, upkeep costs, some end costs, travel and insurance expenses. You could likewise deduct paper costs such as depreciation.

This implies you could acquire a benefit and still depict a paper loss on the tax return. For instance, in reality, you make $2,000 from rental money stream, yet after excluding depreciation, you show a loss on your income-tax return of $3,500. That falls off your taxable income, lessening your expense bill, even though you acquired a benefit.

At the point you sell the property, you could concede taxes on your gains through 1031 exchange. That way, you could continue exchanging upward for properties that create more noteworthy and prominent passive revenue, all without paying a penny in capital gains tax.

7. Diversification

Stock returns are commendable — until a stock exchange amendment renders your stocks collapsing. At that point the normal investor frenzies and sees their stock returns reduce in half.

Real estate signifies a different resource class having a lower correlation to stock returns. Home costs, for the most part, do not fall even in bearish markets, with the striking exemption of the Great Recession. However, that special case demonstrates the standard: The Great Recession was caused in enormous part by a lodging bubble.

Speculators with a diverse arrangement of both the real estate and stocks could lean all the more vigorously on whichever resource class ends up performing better at that point. In 2018, for instance, US stocks encountered a profound revision of almost 20%. However, leases rose by a sound 3.1% as per RENTCafe.

8. Retirement Perks

In the conventional pattern of retirement, you set aside gigantic savings, retire, and then slowly spend down your portfolio. And afterwards, you live off your limited money. That model accompanies a few disadvantages. To start with, you need to figure out a protected withdrawal rate — the level of your portfolio that you could securely pull out each year to spend. Likewise, you should ascertain the amount you need to put aside for retirement, and hit achievements to remain on target to retire by your objective age. In any case, rental property investment would continue creating passive revenue everlastingly.

Limitations of Rental Property Investment

1. Bad Liquidity

With your brokerage fund, you could immediately purchase stocks, mutual funds, ETFs, commodity funds, and other paper resources with a solitary snap. What is more, in this day and age of commission-free brokers, you could do so free of cost. Real estate commonly takes a very long time to purchase or sell. It requires time to research great arrangements on properties before you could purchase. Furthermore, to sell a property, you regularly need to employ an agent and market the property to make sure about a purchaser. Even after agreeing, it still generally takes a month to settle and get your funds. Of course, there are alternate approaches to pull value from a property. However, they include borrowing an amount and generally take a long time to settle.

2. High Obstacles to Entry: Knowledge

Anybody could enlist a monetary guide or robot-counsel to assemble a reasonable stock portfolio for them. On account of robot-counsels, many even deal with your ventures for no cost; for example, SoFi Invest and M1 Finance. No extraordinary information or abilities are required. You simply join, fill in a survey, and let the guide wrap up.

The equivalent cannot be claimed for rental properties. You could put resources into them with fewer risks and higher yields — but just on the off chance that you understand what you are doing.

A couple of the aptitudes that you may require, contingent upon your style of rental contributing, include:

- Picking urban communities and neighborhoods to put resources into
- Discovering great arrangements
- Ascertaining income
- Fund-raising from moneylenders or speculators
- Screening, overseeing, and recruiting contractors
- Screening occupants
- Recruiting and directing property managers

This avoids anything related to the industriousness required once you own a property. At the point when an occupant disregards your rent agreement, you need to register a petition for evacuation, because the cycle typically takes months. Furthermore, when you do not consistently receive rent, you lose more cash, which is hardly recovered again.

3. High Entry Barriers: Capital

You could purchase mutual funds or securities in ETFs for $100. Be that as it may, you cannot accept a property with just a $100 down payment.

Real estate speculators regularly put down somewhere in the range of 20% and 25% when they purchase a property. As per the Federal Reserve, the middle home cost in the US is $327,100. A 20% initial instalment at that point adds up to $65,420, and that does exclude closing costs. It takes cash to bring in cash remains constant in real estate investments.

4. Diversification Challenges

When it costs a huge number of dollars to put resources into a solitary resource, it is difficult to diversify. With $100 speculated into an index reserve, you get exposure to many organizations' securities, perhaps thousands. It renders diversification simple. Compare that with losing $65,420 into a solitary property.

5. Land-lording Headaches

Landowners persevere through unlimited pains from occupants when it comes to the rental property investment. You could outsource a portion, however not all, of the responsibilities to a property manager. Eventually, you would need to deal with the property manager to guarantee that they secure your property and your inclinations.

1.4 Different Types of Rental Properties

Some of the popular types of real rental properties under both commercial and residential zones are as follows. However, the diversities might vary from country to country.

1. Services Apartments

Such an apartment is a top-of-the-line sort of investment property that incorporates all the essential conveniences of a typical apartment, however, has different administrations given by the landowner.

This implies that the serviced apartment incorporates planned cleaning administrations, fixes, house cleaner administrations, and different advantages you may, for the most part, find at an inn. This kind of structure is ideal for people hoping to get a bonus from the arrangement, in addition to all the more likely space, utilities, security, and other facilities. Such an apartment can give the best lavish space to cause the occupant to feel at home, however dissimilar to remaining at the inn; tenants at present might not pay for the utilization of the offices because the rent contract incorporates the whole bundle. Like most condos, in any case, a serviced apartment has private spaces as well as common spaces for all the tenants.

2. Normal Apartments

An apartment in its most essential definition is a leased living space inside a residential structure that differentiates it from a condominium. An ordinary apartment could have at least one rooms, which is ideal for an individual or a family. There could be a few apartment-units in a residential complex. However, every apartment is independent and might be rented or owned. An apartment ought to have all the essential rooms an individual would require, for example, a room, kitchen, and restroom, however, there are different sorts of apartments that incorporate different features and conveniences. A studio apartment, for instance, is ideal for one individual since it just has one room that operates as a dining, living, and bedroom with an attached bath and kitchen. A garden apartment is generally encircled via landscaped regions such as a townhouse, while a loft-apartment comprises of a few units housed inside a multi-story building. The definition may appear to obscure with other kinds of apartments accessible these days; however, most apartment units are normally the studio units suitable for a little family or just an individual.

3. Detached or Street House

A disengaged house is an unattached structure much the same as an ordinary family-possessed house with its private porch, parking region, and a garden. The detached house could likewise be a solitary story or a numerous story structure with different conveniences, for example, a pool, driveway carport and boundary walls. This is diverse to a line house or a roadhouse that are built next to each other with different units. The line house may be a multi-story complex like an apartment, yet they typically have more floor space, and workplaces and shops might take up the lowest levels.

A row house maybe like a high-rise.

However, the last for the most part has a typical territory, and the structure comprises of flights of stairs, lifts, and pathways for everybody. In contrast to houses, the apartments are additionally outfitted with furniture and apparatuses by the landowner, ideal for ex-pats who need to remain in particular countries for a brief timeframe. Similar to villas, the house rentals are intended for long haul stays and for families who need greater spaces for work and study. The houses are additionally significantly less expensive than villas in some countries, even though it is harder to track down houses for lease than the two, villas and apartments, generally.

4. City Villa

A city villa is like a disengaged house or apartment, yet its facilities and luxuries are as a rule of better quality. One key distinction of a city villa from the other rental property classes is the encompassing pool, garden and admittance to different highlights you would typically find in inns.

A villa likewise incorporates a few rooms, garage, furnished kitchen and dining, huge living room, entertainment setup, pool as well as Jacuzzi, and availability to normal zones, for example, the pool, game courts, green, seashore, exercise centres, and others. Some city villas likewise give in-house staff and administrations for a genuinely luxurious encounter. When searching for a villa, think about the area and the closest commercial areas, the highlights mentioned in the agreement, the format, and the unit size.

5. Room Rentals

Room rentals are small-scaled than houses and apartments because the unit comprises just one room like a studio loft. Like any residential space for lease, leasing a room might involve similar essential luxuries, for example, electricity, water, privacy and parking spot. Tenants usually search for rooms that are close to the school and business structures. Landlords need to charge more rent due to the ideal place.

The above may differ in some other countries as follows:

- Single-family houses that are isolated from neighboring properties
- Luxury property-focused toward high-end tenant
- Vacation houses for transient stays
- Row or townhouses that share a gateway, front yard or a connecting wall
- Cooperatives and condos that are exclusive units in a multi-occupant building
- Small multifamily structures, for example, a duplex, trio, or four-plex
- Apartment complexes aimed as high-rise, mid-rise, low-rise or a walk-up

These regular rental property types can likewise have subtypes. For instance, single-family houses can be situated in working-class territories appropriate for labor force inhabitants, condominiums can be planned as lofts or little studio units, and apartment rentals can be ground floor units with admittance to a little garden in a metropolitan setting or a penthouse unit with innumerable luxuries.

Various kinds of investment properties additionally have remarkable advantages and disadvantages. Contingent upon the market you are putting resources into, recent college graduates and families might be eager to pay a higher lease for a solitary family house since they consider the property to be a home that they could live in for quite a long while contrasted with a small apartment.

There are likewise critical contrasts in the development and size, cost of possession and property administration, and the investment/exit methodology among the different sorts of rental property. Commercial rental properties could likewise include spaces and zones for the schools, hospitals, shopping malls, sports complexes and other plaza buildings.

1.5 Most Suitable Real Estate Investment

Although, the decision for what is considered to be the most profitable real estate investment might vary from country to country, or for that matter, from region to region, yet the trends almost follow the likely directions worldwide, at any particular time. In 2020 and past recent years, rental property investment is considered to be the most worthwhile for investors. It is one of the best sources for passive income.

Specifically, in the US, turnkey investment property is a widely endorsed option for investors. A turnkey property is a portion of the property that has been rehabbed and is move-in prepared.

Ordinarily, you would have a property supervisory group taking care of the day-by-day activities, making it a hands-off, passive venture. Turnkey investment property is an incredible investment for the entirety of the reasons. It brings along some exceptional benefits.

If your city has higher real estate costs, such as New York or San Francisco, purchasing investment property might be far off, yet online mediums permit speculators to purchase properties in lower average costs for residential zones. While living far from your investment property, you probably would not deal with the everyday management of the property. Also, you might not be interested in the property administration, but just in the rental inflows. Turnkey investment property organizations usually provide complete administration services, everything from finding the correct property to gathering rent, maintenance along with evicting the tenants.

Purchasing a rental property is not affordable for everybody. Preferably, you would need in any event a 25% down-payment. However, a few commercial centers offer the houses in the low to mid-five figures.

Investors should always make the real estate choice most feasible for them, based on their financial standing, availability of time and other factors.

Chapter 2: Real Property Investment – Risks and Rewards

In case you are thinking about investing resources into real estate property, there is an equivalent proportion of dangers and benefits. Like any speculation, risks could be managed, yet you need to know about them before putting resources into property. Also, similar to any venture, there could be rewards, some very huge.

Real property investment is tied to adjusting risks and rewards. How a speculator adjusts these two aspects relies upon economic situations, his risk-tolerance and certain monetary variables.

Low Reward-Low Risk

Also known as Core speculations, in this class, the speculator is not worried about large gains. Subsequently, the ventures are more secure and yield lower returns. These ventures frequently depend on purchase-and-hold tactics in preferable neighborhoods having properties that require minimal upgrades. They commonly generate a passive revenue where inhabitants have outstanding credit. High rises and business rental properties make great Core speculations.

Moderate Reward-Low Risk

This class of venture is frequently known as Core-Plus. While including purchase-and-hold procedures, these ventures are not exactly as strong. Center Plus spotlights on low-quality properties in reasonable areas, with the creditworthiness of inhabitants being below prime. In certain circumstances, there might be vacancies.

Moderate Reward-Moderate Risk

In this speculation class, the real property speculator looks to increase the value of the property.

Perhaps the landowner tries to improve the property, or a house flipper may remodel a property before selling it. The danger is higher because the speculator is putting cash up past the acquisition cost. There may likewise be a borrowing associated with such ventures, which additionally expands risk. The benefit is generally conceded to the far-end of the undertaking when the landowner could raise rents or house flipper sells off the property for a decent short-period return.

High Reward-High Risk

This procedure includes high forthright speculation with the potential for significant profits; however, there is frequently an extensive stretch with no returns while there are continuous expenses. Ground-up advancements, for example, could go for quite a long time before a return is acknowledged, yet that return could even be 50 %.

There are two contemplations a real property investor ought to consider before entering any speculation. The first of these is the associated disadvantage. Each venture has a drawback. Indeed, even those with different awesome potential gains frequently have, at some rate, one disadvantage. Make certain to remember the drawback when putting resources into real properties. The second thought is the speculator's exit methodology. How would you expect to escape the speculation whenever you have had a gain, or in the improbable occasion when you incur a loss? If you do not consider your exit before you get into a venture, you may end up stuck and accepting bigger misfortunes subsequently. Successful real property speculators figure out how to offset all risk-factors with expected rewards. Investors should not contribute beyond what they could stand to lose.

The following sections are a breakdown of both the advantages and limitations of investing in real estate property.

2.1 Rewards of Real Property Investment

There are various advantages of pooling resources into real properties. With all well-selected resources, investors could merit from expected inflows, magnificent returns, diversifications and tax benefits — and it is conceivable to utilize real properties to generate wealth.

1. Cash Flows

a) Consistent Income

Most investors place assets into real estate for the consistent inflows they acquire as rental receipts. This automated revenue is a gigantic motivation to buy your first real investment property. Depending upon the location and area, investors could generate huge revenues to cover their costs and bring them additional cash as a reconsideration. Metropolitan urban communities or towns having schools and colleges will in general harvest higher rent since the interest in those regions is higher.

When picked carefully, you could make sure about a consistent inflow for long-term and make savings for retirement age. Also, you do not need to refrain from putting assets into each property in turn; you could place resources into different investment properties simultaneously to expand your positive inflows and enhance your real property investment portfolio. Investors could oversee by employing a property management expert if the workload is excessive. Location is vital for smart real property speculation. Remember to select an ideal locality to get the rewards of pooling resources into real estate.

b) Long-Term Financial Security

The merits of pooling resources into real estate endow speculators with long-term monetary security.

At the point when you generate a consistent flow of money progressively, the compensations of such venture bring in long-term monetary rewards. Claiming a rental property could provide security to investors that things are working well due to the property's value appreciation over the long-haul. This implies that your property's estimation would probably rise since the buildings and land are appreciating resources.

Nonetheless, there is no guarantee that property's worth would rise indefinitely. That is why it is prescribed to thoroughly explore the location before finalizing the negotiation on the chosen property.

c) Generate Wealth and Equity

When the property mortgage is paid down, equity is built. Equity is a resource that is included in your asset's net worth. Moreover, as you generate equity, you have the opportunity to purchase more properties and raise even more inflows and wealth.

2. Tax benefits

An advantage of placing resources into real property is the expense exclusions speculators gain from purchasing a speculation property. This is a significant incentive behind why majority decides to put assets into real estates. For instance, rental inflow is exempted from self-employment charge. The investors could enjoy various tax reductions and derivations that can bring about cash savings while paying tax. All in all, you could deduct the relevant expenses of possessing, working, and dealing with a property.

Furthermore, since the expense of purchasing and improving a speculation property could be devalued over its valuable life (27.5 years for private or residential properties; 39 years for business), you profit by many years of allowances that help bring down your taxed inflows.

One fact, however, is that you could charge depreciation on buildings, however not on the land. Another taxation perk is that you might have the option to delay capital-gains by utilizing the 1031 exchange facility. Real property investors are likewise competent for lower tax rates for their long-haul speculations.

3. Inflation Hedge

Real estate investment provides support against inflation. With higher inflation, your rental inflow and property valuation increase altogether. The inflation-hedging capacity of real estate originates from the positive connection between GDP development and real estate's demand. As economies extend, the real estate's demand drives rent upwards. This, thusly, converts into higher capital valuations. Hence, real estate will, in general, keep up the capital's purchasing power by giving a portion of the inflationary strain to occupants and by consolidating a portion of the inflationary weight as capital appreciation. Investors in real estate greet inflation wholeheartedly because as the average cost for basic items goes up, so does their rental income.

4. Appreciation

Being a real estate investor or simply a beginner, you do understand that such a venture is anything but a short-term speculation plan. The benefits of placing resources into real property incorporate the valuation for capital resources (land) over the long run. As such, your property's valuation will be worth much more 35 years from now, thus why speculators are in it for long-term. Real property investors generate inflow through rental revenue, any rewards created by property-based business activities, and appreciation. Real property values, in general increase with the passage of time, and through a wise investment, you could make money when it is an ideal time to sell. Rents additionally, ascent over the long run, in general, which could prompt higher income.

5. Real Property Leverage

Leverage means the utilization of various monetary tools or borrowed capital (e.g., obligation) to raise a speculation's possible return. For instance, a 20% initial mortgage installment grants you 100% of the house you want to buy — that is leverage. Since real estate is a tangible resource and could fill in as security, financing is promptly accessible.

6. Portfolio Diversification

A benefit of venturing money into real estate includes its broadening potential. Real property has a lower — and in certain scenarios inverse — relation with other considerable resource categories. This refers to the notion that inclusion of real estate to the diversified resources' arrangement could reduce the unpredictability and improve the vintage against per unit risk.

7. Combative Risk-Adjusted Inflows

Real property returns differ, contingent upon factors, for instance, resource class, area, and the management. A number that various speculators aim for is to subdue the normal returns of the S&P 500 — what most individuals refer to while stating, "The market." The normal yearly return in the course of recent years is around 11%.

8. Real Estate Investment Trusts (REITs)

In the event that you want to place resources into the estate venture, however, are not prepared to take the leap into overseeing and claiming properties, you would need to ponder over a Real Estate Investment Trust (REIT). You could buy and sell open-market-traded REITs on notable stock markets. Many exchange under higher volume, which implies you could rapidly enter and exit a position. REITs should pay out around 90% of revenue to speculators, so they usually offer higher profits than numerous stocks.

9. You Become Your Decision Maker

Disregard your 9-5 exhausting job, since the best part about real estate is turning into your chief. Much the same as some other business, you have the utter self-rule and power over your real estate venture techniques including your disappointments and triumphs. You give orders on which property to put resources into, the occupants who will live under your rooftop, how much rental revenue to charge every month, and who will oversee and keep up the property overall. The advantages of putting resources into real properties turn you into self-decision-maker.

10. Rental Income Enables Quicker Loan Payoff

At the point when you buy a rental property and take a home loan, the rental stream might have the option to cover the advance installments. This makes managing the property considerably more sensible. At the point when the home loan is fully paid off, the speculator possesses a valuable resource completely paid by the rents the property produced. Being able to fulfil your obligation much quickly is a significant benefit of real estate investments. In case you could generate positive income and have the property pay for itself through the rents, you would have a more noteworthy possibility for an effective venture.

Without a doubt, the real estate market is a worthwhile business for numerous entrepreneurs and speculators. Many perceive the advantages of resource investment into real estate to receive long-term monetary benefits and financial security. Regardless of the numerous benefits of pooling resources into real properties, there are limitations as well. One fundamental drawback is the lack of liquidity (or the overall trouble in converting over a resource into cash and cash into a resource).

Unlike a bond or stock exchange, which could be completed in short order, a real property transaction could take a long period to close. Even with the help of a merchant, it could take several weeks to locate a suitable counterparty.

Real estate market is still an unmistakable resource category that is easier to comprehend and could improve the danger-and-return portrait of a speculator's portfolio. The real property offers tax reductions, income, value building, combative risk-adjusted revenues, and an inflation hedge. It could thereby enhance a portfolio by narrowing down unpredictability through diversification, regardless of whether you place assets into REITs or physical properties.

2.2 Risks of Real Property Investment

There are numerous dangers associated with real estate investment that must be considered in addition to the normal estimation of the venture. Having the criteria for speculators to evaluate risks ensures that the speculation coordinates with their necessities, tolerance and objectives.

Here are different risk factors which investors ought to consider while assessing any real estate speculation:

1. Real Estate Market's Unpredictability

Real estate industry has been developing very well over the previous few years; notwithstanding, there is no assurance that this positive pattern will proceed. The real estate market is popular for its high points and low points with the always-changing financial conditions. In real investment, the economy assumes a significant part in the estimation of a venture property. In this way, there is no assurance that investors would earn a benefit when they choose to sell a speculation property.

For instance, when you purchase venture properties during the period when demand for real estate investment is high, you may be at the danger of selling them for lower than the underlying price tag (regardless of whether this property created benefit through rental inflows) since its worth has gone down as the lodging market changes. This might cost you more cash than what you have acquired while leasing the property.

Thus, while entering the real estate business, investors ought to know about this dynamic, comprehend and remain updated with the market economy and how it works, and predict any downturns in real estate market beforehand. This would assist them with deciding if purchasing a venture property at a specific time is a wise speculation choice.

2. Negative Cash Flows

In real properties investment, the income from venture properties is the measure of benefit that the property speculator acquires in the wake of taking care of all costs, taxes, and home loan installments. The subsequent risk related to real investment is the chance of producing a negative inflow rather than a positive one. This implies that costs, taxes and duties, and mortgage installments are altogether higher than the rental revenues, which leads to losing cash.

The negative income risk occurs when the property speculator purchases venture properties without leading the market investigation first. Subsequently, the ideal approach to keep away from this danger is by precisely figuring your revenue and costs (how much the rental inflows will be and the amount you would need to spend on the property) before purchasing a speculation property. Also, ensure that the investment property is situated in an ideal locality that yields positive income, to ensure a high yield on a venture. It is essential to be very careful since, in real estate investment, even the minute costs may accumulate over the long haul.

3. Unsuitable Locations

Location is significant in real estate investment. Knowledgeable speculators concur that when you are purchasing any venture properties, the area should consistently be the prime factor to ponder over. In what manner would the location be able to be a danger in estate investments? There are a few manners by which putting resources into a bad locality would prompt ineffective real estate speculation.

To start with, area decides the demand and supply. You may think a specific area is a decent decision for investment because of lower costs. Nonetheless, these areas could have a large number of venture properties accessible but not have a developing populace or a great job market. Accordingly, putting resources into these locations would cause speculators extraordinary risks.

Besides, the property speculators ought to dodge areas that have a moderately higher crime percentage. From one viewpoint, these territories have lower costs and high inhabitance rate since individuals would in general lease rather than purchase homes. Moreover, when pooling resources into high crime zones, the investors might confront the danger of getting vandalized or ransacked, which would prompt unexpected costs along with high repairing costs, together with the hardships of legal issues consequently.

Besides, in real property investment, location decides value appreciation. Low appreciation implies a negative rate of profitability when the property speculator chooses to sell a venture property. Accordingly, property investors should never purchase speculation properties merely dependent on price.

An ideal tactic to keep away from such risks is for speculators to be cautious while picking the area for real property investment. Although it might be enticing to buy a modest venture property, by and large, the risk is not justified, despite any potential benefits.

4. Leverage Risk

The more obligation on speculation, the higher risk it has and the higher investors should demand as a return. Leverage implies the force multiplier: it could carry a project along rapidly and increase the surplus when things are working out positively, however, if a venture's credits are under pressure – normally when its profit from resources is not sufficient to cover revenue installments – investors would, in general, lose faster and a great deal.

Leverage ought not to surpass 75% since this sort of obligation must be fulfilled before the common equity. Returns should be created principally from the real estate operations – not through unnecessary utilization of leverage – and speculators must comprehend this point. Usually, property speculators do not understand that it is so essential to measure leverage, so they end up in over-geared ventures. Speculators ought to get some information about how much leverage is utilized to underwrite an asset and guarantee that they are getting a return equivalent with the involved risk.

5. Tenant Issues

Getting occupants is a need for bringing in cash in real estate investments. Nonetheless, merely getting any occupant would not ensure profitability. The risk of getting troublesome inhabitants and stalling out with them could be far more atrocious than the danger of not having an occupant by any stretch of the imagination.

While it is true that not having occupants implies not generating any rental inflow. Notwithstanding, intolerant occupants may decline to pay the lease for a while in succession, or even decimate the property to an extreme, which means you would have to manage evacuations – which are both expensive and tedious.

To stay away from the danger of having uncompromising tenants, property investors should try choosing good tenants cautiously. Leading an exhaustive occupant screening measure, checking their credit rating, and approaching them for contact data of their past landlord might be some helpful initiatives.

6. Absence of Liquidity

Liquidity is the capacity to get to the cash you have inside a venture. One danger of real estate is that real venture properties are illiquid, which means you could only with significant effort convert them into money. Selling a property is neither a speedy nor a basic process, whereas selling under pressure or rapidly would no doubt bring about writing off your venture.

This absence of liquidity renders the speculators to hold their ventures for more time than other kinds of ventures, which is a risk for the individuals who might require admittance to money rapidly if essential.

7. Vacancy Risks

Purchasing a speculation property does not consequently ensure 100% inhabitance and brisk benefits. In real properties investment, there is the chance of a greater vacancy, which is a significant danger to investors' rental revenue as it could yield negative income.

Additionally, since inhabitants are the means of rental inflow in estate investments, vacancy is a colossal danger for speculators who depend on rental inflow to take care of their insurance, mortgage, property taxes, and different costs.

To retain a strategic distance from the risks of high vacancy, real estate speculators should buy venture properties in a decent location having higher demand. These areas are usually protected neighborhoods with close by enhancements, for example, transportation, shopping centres, and schools.

8. Concealed Structural Problems

In real properties investment, a property speculator might wind up purchasing a venture property with genuine hidden structural issues, which builds the odds of confronting sudden repairs and upkeep costs.

To stay away from such trouble, get a property appraisal and a decent assessment of the condition of a speculation property before you even purchase the investment property. Property appraisers are experts who would have the option to find any concealed harms or issues that need fixing; moreover, they would reveal to you precisely how much your potential venture property is worth.

9. Depreciation

In real property investment, depreciation is something contrary to appreciation. Generally, real properties are considered to increase in worth throughout the long term (appreciation). Notwithstanding, not all properties are ensured to rise in worth. Consequently, a significant danger of real property investment is putting resources into an investment property whose worth drops later on, which means the property speculators would wind up losing cash.

Indeed, an ideal approach to maintain a strategic distance from the depreciation risk is to be cautious in your exploration and real property market examination as well as study the monetary development of the land market to discover an area with a solid positive real property appreciation.

10. Time

Putting resources into real properties needs a great deal of exploration to be done before you settle on any choice. Putting resources into real estate is the time game. You need to dedicate a great deal of extra time to do your exploration concerning the type of property you need to put resources into if you are going for the private or business property. Many speculators cannot traverse their arrangements of putting resources into real estate since they do not have much time close by to contribute. Some investors begin with great energy, yet as time passes by; they begin losing interest and eventually surrender.

Real property market turns out to be one of the slowest developing business sectors. Estate prices barely increase overnight. More often than not, the real estate price remains precisely the same even after years which implies that the cash you have ventured by putting resources into real properties is losing its worth.

11. Capital

Real estate investment is presumably one of those ventures that require a gigantic measure of capital. You could not accept any property, be it private or business without having the required capital. Many individuals who are low on capital want to go for bank borrowing, which implies that their end cost would be high since they would be paying to the bank or organization before their loan. Many investors opt the mortgage option and wind up paying all the lease for their monthly contract, which implies that regardless of what course they pick, real estate speculation relies on capital.

12. Investment into Foreign Capital

Individuals generally for the sake of speculation, prefer purchasing a property in foreign nations, thinking of it as an insightful move; there are a lot of hindrances and dangers associated with such activity. The tax assessment framework for investing resources into the host nation often differs from that in abroad. There is a huge documentation work included which could be overwhelming.

There are also various political risks which could render it hard for investors to keep up the property in an unfamiliar country. With the change in political authority, for example, from being a fully democratic nation to a partly democratic one, the terms and states of owing a property could substantially change. Resale of the property is likewise another significant issue with regards to purchasing a property in the far-off nation.

Real estate speculators ought to investigate all such risks and get straight responses to be more certain about their investment choices. They should know about any speculation chances that do not make all the included risks crystal clear.

Chapter 3: Real Properties for Beginners

While putting assets into real estate, the objective is to invest cash today and permit it to expand with the goal that you have more cash later on. The benefit, or return, you make on your ventures should adequately cover the taxes you pay, risks taken, and different expenses of possessing the estate, for example, utilities, insurance and maintenance.

Real estate venture for the starters could truly be as basic as playing Monopoly, once they comprehend the essential variables of the venture, risks and financial matters. To win, you purchase properties, maintain a strategic distance from insolvency, and produce rental inflows to purchase considerably more properties. Nonetheless, remember that "basic" does not signify "easy." If you commit an error, the results could go from minor burdens to serious fiascos.

Having speculations in the mutual funds or securities exchange could be vital to your monetary future. Nonetheless, it must be done rationally and should be begun ahead of schedule to avail compounding interest's benefit. Many investors might have considered real estate as another venture instrument. It is an ideal method to assemble the establishment of a sound monetary future. Much like a conventional investment, there are significant incentives for beginning promptly in life. It is likewise the most misjudged approaches to invest.

We have all observed individuals create wealth on appreciation or found out about individuals who went from being debtors to millionaires utilizing no-cash-down methodologies. Without doubt, real estate speculating is perhaps the ideal approaches to bring in cash in both the long and short run.

The explanation is basic – it is a generally safe venture with high potential for return and development. Nonetheless, similar to any start, beginning with property ventures could appear to be an overwhelming task. Nevertheless, the main thing to comprehend is that the advantages of real estate are not selective to seasoned capitalists. There are a few methodologies on estate investing for amateurs that could assist anybody with the beginning.

Like any speculation chance, there are sure dangers associated with real estate. Be that as it may, by setting aside the effort to get to know the market investors could help guarantee they keep from regular errors. Regardless of whether you intend to seek after speculating full time or as a side hustle, real property investment has demonstrated its productivity consistently.

Real properties investment could be intimidating for the inexperienced ones in the business. It could take some time (or properties) before financial specialists become completely agreeable in estate investment. That is the reason beginner-friendly investment procedures are a decent beginning stage. While they are reasonable for speculators with little insight, they could, in any case, be profoundly beneficial when overseen accurately.

Beginning in a novice-friendly speculating niche is an incredible method to get familiar with the ropes before taking on more unpredictable ventures. By beginning with an available procedure to start, speculators could become acquainted with their neighborhood market, assemble a network and figure out how to raise capital without focusing on an arrangement they might not be prepared to deal with. Investors would then be able to utilize their experience and gains, to progress into different procedures down the line.

3.1 Real Estate Investment – Important Factors

Contrasted with different kinds of ventures, real estate investment includes a moderately approving risk/rewards profile, with generally low liquidity (easy entrance and exit). While the area is consistently a key aspect, various variables help decide whether real speculation is appropriate for you. Here is a gander at the main factors while you intend to put resources into the real property market.

1. The Sort of Property you need to Prefer

There are different categories of real properties. These are industrial, residential, retail and business zones. The residential estate is the most secure sort to put resources into. The reason is that the pace of return is in a real sense ensured. One of the fundamental human necessities is shelter and individuals would consistently look for homes to dwell into. Subsequently, you would undoubtedly get inhabitants for your residential properties.

Nonetheless, residential land has a lower net revenue when contrasted with different kinds. Business, industrial and retail properties offer a more critical net revenue. In any case, there is a lot higher danger of no rent payment or vacancy during intense economic occasions. Consequently, it is essential to realize which kind of property you mean to put resources into as you think about this endeavor.

2. Property's Locality

Why is it Crucial?

The maxim that area is the key is as yet a ruler and keeps on being the main factor for profitableness in real properties investment.

Nearness to facilities, scenic vistas, green space and the locale's status are noticeable factors into residential property's valuations. Closeness to business sectors, stockrooms, and transport centres, roads, and tax-exempt territories assume a significant function in business property valuations.

What to Quest For?

A key while considering property area is the mid-to-long-haul view concerning how the territory is anticipated to develop over the speculation time frame. For instance, the present tranquil open land at the rear of a residential structure could sometimes turn into a noisy factory unit, decreasing its worth. Investors should thoroughly analyze the possession and expected use of the prompt regions where they intend to invest.

One approach to gathering data about the likelihoods of the property location you are thinking about is to contact the city center or other public offices responsible for zoning and metropolitan arranging. This would give you admittance to the long-haul region arranging and make an assurance on how positive or troublesome your property plan is.

3. Investment Horizon and Venture Purpose

Why is it Significant?

Considering the high-value and low liquidity venture in real estate, an absence of clearness might prompt unexpected outcomes, including monetary distress — particularly if the venture is mortgaged.

What to Search For?

Distinguish which of the accompanying general classifications suits your incentives, and afterwards plan appropriately:

- **Purchasing and self-utilization:** Here, you would save money on lease and have the advantage of self-usage, while likewise getting appreciation in value.

- **Purchasing and renting:** This offers consistent revenue and long-haul value appreciation. Notwithstanding, the personality to be a landowner is expected to deal with potential legal issues and disputes, oversee occupants, maintenance works and other activities.

- **Purchasing and selling (short-haul):** This is by and large for rapid, little to medium gains when the property is under erection and sold at a gain upon completion.

- **Purchasing and selling (long-haul):** This is commonly centered on huge internal worth appreciation over an extensive stretch. This approach offers choices complementary with long-haul objectives, for example, retirement.

4. Property Valuation

Why is it Important?

Property valuation is significant for financing during price listing, purchasing, venture analysis, tax assessment and insurance — they all rely upon real property valuation.

What to Search For?

Generally utilized real property valuation strategies include:

- **Sales Contrasting Approach:** This strategy includes the latest comparable deals of properties with identical qualities. It is similar and appropriate for both new and old properties.

- **Cost Approach:** Here, the expense of the land and development, minus depreciation is considered. It is reasonable for new development.

- **Revenue Approach:** This strategy incorporates expected money inflows and is appropriate for rentals.

5. Anticipated Profit Opportunities and Cash Flows

Why is it Important?

Inflow alludes to how much cash is left after incurring costs. Positive inflow is vital to a decent return rate for a speculation property.

What to Look For?

- Create projections for the accompanying methods of costs and profits:

- Expected income from rental inflows (inflation favors landowners for rental revenue)

- The anticipated rise in intrinsic worth about long-haul value appreciation

- Advantages of depreciation (plus accessible tax reliefs)

- Cost-benefit evaluation of renovating before the sale for better pricing

- Cost-benefit analysis of value appreciation versus mortgaged loans

6. Your Present Credit Score

Your credit rating ordinarily influences the kind of home loan you get. This score is a significant component which influences the borrowing rate that you get for your home loans. Only a couple of points above or below your credit score could render a significant impact on your mortgage. Consequently, before you take out a home loan as an element of putting resources into private real estate, assure that your credit score is favorable. If it is all right, then you could proceed-otherwise, figure out how to raise it.

What to Expect?

Scores more than 800 are viewed as highly favorable and would assist you with qualifying for the best home loan. If important, deal with improving your credit rating:

- Cover tabs on schedule — set up programmed installments or updates
- Pay down obligation
- Aim for close to 30% credit usage (not higher)
- Unused credit cards should not be closed — if as you are not paying yearly charges
- Demands for hard inquiries and new requests should be limited
- Examine your dispute inaccuracies and credit report

7. Be Cautious with Leverage

Why is it Important?

Bank loans are helpful. However, they might come at a major expense. One commits their prospective revenue to get utility at present at the expense of interest spread across several years. Be certain that you know how to deal with credits of this nature and maintain a strategic distance from elevated levels of obligation or over-leverage. Indeed, specialists in real estate are tested by over-leverage amid adverse economic situations, and the liquidity deficiencies with high obligation commitments could break real properties ventures.

What to Look For?

Contingent on your current and anticipated future income, think about the following:

- Settle on the sort of home loan that best accommodates your circumstance — adjustable-rate mortgage (ARM), fixed-rate, zero down installment, interest-only and other categories. Note that each kind of home loan has its danger profile, and you need to examine each cautiously. For example, ARM incorporates contract rates that could change whenever driven by capital market influences, and the borrower should acknowledge any rate changes during the borrowing term.

- Know about terms, conditions, and different charges collected by the home loan moneylender.

- Shop around to discover better terms and lower loan charges.

8. Indirect Speculations in Real Estate

Why is it Important?

Overseeing actual properties over a long-haul plan is not for everybody. Options exist that permit you to speculate funds into the estate area indirectly.

What to Look For?

Think about alternate approaches to put assets into real estate:

- Real estate venture trusts

- Real estate organization stocks

- Real estate area-centered mutual assets and ETFs

- Home loan bonds

- Mortgage-supported securities

9. Existing Property versus New Construction

Why is it Important?

New development normally offers alluring prices, the choice to modify, and advanced services. Dangers incorporate deferrals, increased expenses, and the uncertainties of a recently evolved neighborhood. Existing properties provide convenience, quicker access, upgradations (landscaping, utilities and others), and mostly, lower costs.

What to Look For?

Here are some important aspects to search for when settling on a new development or a current property:

- Survey past activities and explore the development organization's standing for new speculations.

- Audit property deeds, evaluation reports and recent surveys for existing properties.

- Consider monthly upkeep costs, taxes, and accrued expenses. Such costs could seriously affect your income.

- When putting resources into a rented property, see whether the property is lease-stabilized, lease-controlled or free market. Is the rent going to lapse? Are reestablishment choices good for the occupant? Who claims the furnishings?

- Quality-check things (furniture, equipment and installations) if these are to be incorporated for the deal.

10. The Current State of the Real Market

Conditions in the property alter frequently. While you sell a house, high property costs are a favorable condition. However, if the property costs are low, it is an ideal opportunity to purchase instead of selling. Considering such factors, before pooling resources into any real property, carry out some exploration around that region to discover the prevalent market situations. They are a significant component of a real estate venture.

11. Your Revenues should be Steady

Putting resources into real estate is a monetary responsibility. At first, it could take more from you than it offers in return.

In this way, you need to guarantee that you have a steady income to assist you to survive the monetarily testing period between your buying and selling of a property. A dependable guideline is to check whether you are working with excess money. Likewise, make a monetary projection of the following half-year of your life. Would your inflows still be steady during that period? If so, then at such point you are monetarily sound enough to make real estate speculation. If not, settle your finances first.

12. The Attributes of the Property

The condition of the structure which you plan to purchase is a fundamental aspect to consider. Appealing houses or areas of land are typically encircled by the decent foundation, for instance, tarmac roads, street lamps, good seepage frameworks and well-constructed pavements. Likewise, alluring houses commonly have structural integrity, decent layout, a wide floor design and facilities, for example, galleries and grilling spots in the open-air porch. Such specifications should be looked for while considering a real estate venture. This is because the features of a house or a plot of land could attract or repulse occupants. Accordingly, opt the property which has appealing highlights to create good returns.

13. The Kind of Occupant

Relatively few residential real estate speculators consider the kind of inhabitant they need. Many need the one who pays their lease timely. There is significantly more to an inhabitant than simply having the option to pay their lease on schedule. The kind of inhabitant whom you acknowledge is a significant component to consider. It would help if you are looking for an occupant who has a decent rental history, is disciplined, mature and honest. You could arrange to talk with occupants before you permit them to live in your property. This guarantees that you would have an issue-free residential venture.

14. Consider the Views of Your Desired Occupant

In marketing, the client is right in every scenario. This rule additionally applies to the real property market. In case you are undertaking a house construction for renting or selling it out, focus on your objective occupant's perspective first. Figure out what would appeal them and afterwards follow that in your development. In case you are placing resources into the real property market for selling it subsequently, you could likewise consider this element. What would a prospective buyer admire about it? This would assist you with making strategic enhancements which would pull in buyers and ensure you a desired return.

15. Real Estate Legislations

Before you carry out a significant venture, you should be acquainted with the laws of the region you are buying a property in, just as the duties you would be paying. In such cases, it is rational to recruit a legal advisor who knows about the intricate details to help acclimate you with the whole cycle and the strategies that should be followed to abstain from paying fines or ending up in an awkward circumstance, particularly with regards to taxes.

3.2 Ways for Real Estate Investment

Purchasing and claiming real estate is a speculation methodology that could be both fulfilling and rewarding. Unlike stock and bond speculators, imminent estate proprietors could utilize leverage to purchase a property by paying a segment of the complete cost forthright, subsequently paying the balance off, along with interest, over the long haul.

While a customary home loan, by and large, requires a 20% to 25% initial installment, at times a 5% initial installment is everything necessary to buy a whole property.

This capacity to control the resource instantly as documents are signed encourages both land flippers and landowners, who could, then, take out second home loans on their homes to pay installments on extra properties.

Following are the ways for real estate investment with and without purchasing the property.

Ways to Invest in Real Estate by Buying Property?

1. Purchase and Fix Up a House

Flipping a house is as primary as you could get for a venture. You purchase the property, put assets into setting it up, and then sell it at a gain. Fixing a home needs funds past the underlying venture and additional time than you might have. It is a cycle and one that requires strong information on home improvement and real estate. Indeed, even profiting flips could seem as outflows for some time. Tolerance is essential in case you want to focus on a fixer-upper.

2. Purchase Rental Property

This could mean various things. Principally, if you possess the cash, you could buy a whole investment property and lease any room or loft to inhabitants. Minimize your costs so you could keep lease moderate to lure planned occupants.

You likewise could buy a property that you live in while leasing different rooms in the property. In any case, you are the property manager. Being a decent one would greatly improve your situation to prevail in the given speculation. Keep the property in extraordinary condition, be promptly accessible to your inhabitants when required, and if important recruit somebody who could assist with fixes.

3. Lease-to-Own a Home

Lease-to-claim is where you sign an agreement to lease a home for a foreordained timeframe with the alternative to buy the home once that time lapses.

Regularly, that choice is a prerequisite- a guarantee that you would purchase the home. Some percentage of your lease installments per month constitute the down-payment on a home loan when the buying gets official.

Lease-to-possess arrangements accompany risks. However, they are useful for individuals who could not presently focus on purchasing a home. This provides individuals with different advances (medical bills, credit card outstanding and others) an ideal opportunity to pay those off without the additional monetary incidence of a periodic mortgage. Go through the rent-to-own contract thoroughly to ensure the included content is favorable for you, and it could help you slide your way into a venture.

4. Buy Vacation Property

A vacation property implies leasing to inhabitants for more limited periods. Keeping a maintained house in the correct territory might get you the option to bring in similar cash off a couple of vacation occupants that you might make from an all-year inhabitant somewhere else. Vacation rentals, since they are so regularly in an attractive territory, could be costly both to purchase and keep up. Investors should gauge the advantages and disadvantages of cautiously. Upon doing it right - they should research thoroughly and hire good agents - a seashore rental could be worthwhile for summers.

5. Buy Non-Residential, Commercial Property

Business property - retail structures or places of business - is a fascinating alternative for the individuals who need to put resources in real estate past the residential property. It is dearer, and you might need to search for accomplices in this speculation.

As an owner or part-proprietor of the property, you could lease it out to organizations needing space.

It is high-risk-reward real estate contributing. Inflows generated from leasing space to organizations is commonly higher than that from inhabitants, and usually, the agreements to rent business structures are longer than private ones.

6. Utilize Lodging Applications as Airbnb

Airbnb has become a mainstream path for several property owners to enhance their inflows. Why not consolidate it into your venture? For Airbnb to function, register your home on the application, indicate the kind of housing you are offering (you could offer a room or the whole property), the number of individuals it could oblige and its accessibility. You would additionally approve the visitors remaining at your property.

Airbnb could be a decent decision in specific zones. You might have the option to make a respectable benefit utilizing Airbnb. In case it is a property you own yet do not dwell in; the additional accessibility could assist a lot.

7. Purchase Your House

Instead of purchasing a house explicitly to flip it, purchasing and holding could at times be coincidental to why you purchased the house: to live there. However, reliably paying your home loan and doing general upkeep for the house to create upgrades could raise the valuation of your home, should you one day search for another spot to live. Deal with your home like a long-term venture, and it might compensate down the line.

Real Estate Investment without Buying Property

1. Investment into Real Estate Investment Trusts (REITs)

A REIT, or real estate speculation trust, is an organization that either claims or funds real property that produces inflows. REITs put most of their cash into real estate, and it is how they generate most of their revenues. Some REITs emphasize on both private and business property.

Most REITs are equity-based, yet some exchange mortgages rather than actual properties. A generally significant aspect for the estate speculators is that minimum 90% of the taxable revenue it delivers is through dividends to the investors. So, analyzing flourishing REITs and buying securities in them is potentially a productive venture.

2. Real Estate ETFs Investing

Notwithstanding REITs, there exist REIT ETFs or stock market-traded assets. REITs put resources into real estate; REIT ETFs put resources into REITs. It very well might be safer than putting straightforwardly in a REIT, and safer than physically purchasing property, yet you would likewise be getting, to a lesser extent, a return back. In any case, if the risk is perhaps the greatest concern while thinking about estate speculation, a REIT ETF is an approach that should be thought of.

3. Investing in Real Estate Mutual Funds

These funds vary, to some degree, from REITs. Though a REIT is a real organization, mutual funds are merely ventures pooled together and directed by a speculation administrator.

Mutual funds permit real estate speculators to expand their portfolio both regarding having a real estate and a mutual fund. As with different kinds of shared assets, you could pick the ones that are revenue-oriented or growth-oriented. As a diversified resource, they are developed with the expectation of moderating risk, yet they are as yet defenseless against the real estate inherent risk. If a risk associated with real estate adversely influences one of the ventures in the mutual fund, it would probably affect many others as well.

4. Wholesaling Houses

Wholesaling real property is somewhat like flipping homes. However, you do not possess the home, and you do not need to bear any up-keep cost. Wholesaling a house implies contracting somebody willing to sell their home, and rapidly taking that agreement and offering it to a planned purchaser for a gain, which the distributor keeps. No repairing is included in this approach.

It would be favorable if you could successfully manage so. There is substantially less danger since you are not placing your cash into the activity. The troublesome portion of doing this is finding an undervalued house that you could potentially sell for a gain.

5. Real Estate Partnerships

Some real estate speculations require a significant measure of capital. Not every investor could afford that. In case you are not the only one engaged with the speculation, by any means, it could turn out to be more reasonable. Partnerships are a typical method to put resources into real estate, with every individual taking over various duties. Usually, this could be utilized as an approach to buy property at a lower cost. You could set the terms, for example, just paying the home loan, or maybe taking care of the up-front installment for the property. Contingent upon the provisions of your association, you might be putting resources into a real property without doing much active work of claiming property.

6. Utilize an Online Real Estate Speculation Platform

Just as with different kinds of stocks, there are online mediums that help you make real estate speculations too. Frequently, these speculations you make are included in crowdfunding- a route for others to have the option to purchase property without requiring funding.

This choice would, in general, be more for those with cash to save, considering the costs important to buy the huge property.

7. Speculate into Real Estate Service Organizations

Many companies operate essentially in the realm of real properties that you could put resources into. Look past REITs for your real estate organizations. For instance, RE/MAX is an organization that sells homes with the assistance of realtors. Organizations engaged with real properties that do not include purchasing property could be an approach to enhance your portfolio as well as get a decent sense of the present estate market.

8. Becoming a Real Estate Appraiser

Have you thought about a job inside the real estate business? It could not exclusively be speculation of sorts, however, could set you up for how the market is getting along, and when all is good and well, to make wise ventures.

One job position inside the business to consider is that of a real property appraiser. An appraiser could have practical experience in either private or business property, and decide the valuation of a property. They consider particulars about both the property and its close by environmental factors to do this. As signified by the U.S. Department of Labor Statistics (BLS), the median compensation for a real property appraiser or assessor in May 2017 was $54,010. Those with the most significant compensations could make over $101,000 per year.

9. Speculate into House Construction Companies

Another real property-related speculation that could merit your time includes organizations that are associated with home construction.

There are a lot of home construction organizations whose securities trade on the NYSE regularly, for example, Horton (DHI) and Lennar (LEN). It is an appealing speculation alternative for the individuals who accept that the development of homes is a sector that would keep on expanding.

10. Initiate a Brokerage or Be an Estate Agent

You could likewise get into selling the real estate. Realtors require some training and education before they could enter the market and flip houses; yet, fruitful realtors could bring home decent commissions on the properties they sell.

Agents, by and large, work for estate brokers, and while you would preferably be at the leading position instead of selling the homes, you might think about starting a brokerage and recruiting agents. Estate brokerages get a huge portion of the commission that the agents generate, thus having effective agents could acquire a significant amount of money.

However, initiating a brokerage is not straightforward, and is staggeringly costly. You need licenses and extensive training to open and look after one. In case you are an effective agent searching for the succeeding stage in your real estate profession, it very well might be rational thought. However, if you have not reached there yet, in terms of success, information or financing, you might want to begin turning into an agent.

3.3 Is Real Property Investment Worthwhile?

Generally, real estate is an extraordinary venture choice. It could create continuous passive revenue and could be a satisfactory long-term venture if the value increases over the long haul. You might even consider it as a fragment of your general tactic to start generating wealth.

In any case, you need to be confident that you are ready to begin investing resources into the estate market. For one, you should put down huge sum forthright to begin real estate speculation. Purchasing a home, high rise, or land patch could be costly. There would also be the routine maintenance expenses you would incur, along with potential revenue gaps while you are between inhabitants for a period.

Some real estate speculators start by buying a house or a duplex with portions and living in one unit while leasing the other out. This is a decent strategy to consider going all in, however, remember that you would be living in a similar structure as your occupant. Also, when you compose your financial plan, you would need to ensure you could cover the whole home loan and yet live peacefully without additional lease installments coming in.

Once you get more consistent being a landowner and dealing with a speculation property, you might think about purchasing a bigger property with more revenue potential. When you own few properties, it gets easier to buy and administer more properties, plus generate a more reasonable return from your ventures.

What is your Real Estate Investment Goal?

If you believe purchasing an investment property is a simple method to broaden your stock portfolio and gather a steady income each month without making the slightest effort, you would be dismayed. Then again, if you need to develop your wealth dramatically within a couple of years, that is unthinkable in the securities exchange. You do not have the control, and there is no predictable method to win a deal regardless of your long-hours research.

However, with real properties, if you are determined for the hard-work, your net value could go twofold, triple, or fourfold in a generally short measure of time. Therefore, assess your objectives.

What sort of profits are you searching for? Do you need passive revenue (and lower Return on Investment), or do you have the energy and time to devote to establishing a genuine real property business?

With everything taken into account, on the off chance that you are a business person who has not yet wandered into real estate contributing, it is worthwhile to consider doing so. The reason is that many have found out about real estate's reliably rewarding ROI's in practically every market — a venture that would keep on giving, even notwithstanding the present economic vulnerability.

Everybody needs someplace to live. This is a motivation behind why multi-family land could, in any case, pay effective returns even during a pandemic. Presently, the rental market is flourishing, and you might discover extraordinary arrangements during an emergency, which implies now could be an ideal chance to think about real estate investment. Especially when an estate market has a populace development, job growth and affordability, you would probably have the option to discover wise investment openings.

Chapter 4: Real Property- The Practical Aspects

By now, we have learned that putting resources into real properties is one of the sharpest cash moves you could make. Whether you are investing in a solitary family home for yourself or to use as an investment property or purchasing multi-family private property, it is a steady and safe venture. It is a shrewd move to get ready for retirement utilizing a blend of various speculations, involving real estate.

Unlike putting resources into the financial exchange, putting resources into real estate implies that you generally have the actual resource to represent for your costs. Real estate speculation for starters might appear to be overpowering. However, it does not need to be. Continue perusing the upcoming sections for the real properties' know-how to help you get started.

4.1 Why to Invest in Rental Properties?

Possessing an investment property is only one of the numerous approaches to accomplish the goal of generating huge cash. An experienced rental property speculator realizes that it gives the best of the results. Here are some persuading reasons behind claiming an investment in rental properties.

1. Low Vacancy Risks

The rental estate is sound in almost every corner of the world, and there is no deficiency of imminent inhabitants. What is more, regardless of whether the economy thoroughly falls, individuals are continually going to require a spot to live. In financial downturns, rentals are frequently more popular as fewer individuals could stand to purchase a home.

2. Security and Control

One significant advantage of rental property ventures is that you are in charge of what property to put resources into, where it is found, whom to lease to and what to charge for lease. You have next to no control when putting resources into the financial exchange and numerous different speculations. Putting resources into real estate is likewise viewed as one of the most secure ventures you could make. Contrasted with the instability of the financial exchange, estate markets would, in general, be very steady. It is imperative to remember this while picking between putting resources into the estates versus stocks.

3. High Return on Investments (ROI)

When you borrow cash for property venture, you are placing a little part of your cash to put resources into that property. You would improve return on your speculation eventually. What is more, as market influences keep on driving rents higher, rental property investors would be in a real spotlight.

Once more, the lease will consistently cover both peripheral costs and further take care of the interest on your borrowings. In such a circumstance, your gain would go past a few sorts of speculations — it would outperform the owed interest, and that is an expansion in ROI. With higher leverage as expressed before, your monthly revenue would rise, bringing about a higher ROI.

4. Retire on Rental Revenues

The possibility to retire on rental inflows gives a decent outlook about the market; it is additionally a good means for passive revenue. You could possess a rental property business for quite a long time, raise the net worth and use the income in supporting a retirement reserve — or even satisfy your home-loan with rental inflows.

5. Appreciation

Rental properties, in general, appreciate in worth with the time, which implies that while you are gathering cash as a lease, you could watch the worth go up. You could benefit from the passive revenue while taking care of the home-loan, afterwards sell the property at a greater price and benefit from it once more.

6. Inflows

Any cash left after paying your monthly costs is cash in your pocket. Purchase savvy, and you could produce a monthly revenue from your inhabitants as lease far over what it expenses to possess the property. This is money in your pocket that you could enjoy for however long you own and lease your property.

7. Tax Advantages

There are numerous tax benefits of putting resources into rental properties. On the off chance that you get a rental payment, there are various rental costs you may deduct on your tax returns. Costs may incorporate mortgage interest, operating costs, property tax, repairs and depreciation. There are many tax relaxations – be certain to talk with your tax professional to assure you comprehend all tax inferences before speculating resources into a rental property.

8. Leverage

One significant advantage to focus on is leverage. You could utilize a small portion of your cash while borrowing. When putting resources into rental estates, you do not need to pay everything for the property. You could put an initial installment (even as low as 0%) of your cash and get a credit from a bank, private loan specialist or a moneylender to support the leftover. While you merely invest a small level of your cash in the property, you could completely control the rental property and advantage from 100% appreciation.

9. Sweat Equity

Another factor that you ought to ponder over is that more value-addition from your sweat equity would occur from the enhancements made in the property as you keep up and redesign it. Doing things like adding new siding, repainting the home, revamping within, doing some essential finishing to the yard would enhance the home without critical monetary expense. Not exclusively would this permit you to charge more for lease, it will likewise raise the estimation of the property itself should you decide to sell it later on.

If you prefer home improvement activities, this should be a significant fascination for purchasing a rental property. You will have the chance for fixing it up upon obtaining just as in between the occupants, which will restore immense profits for you.

10. Sell Whenever

The rental property market also provides you with a chance to sell when you need to and however you want. In any case, specialists would encourage you to clutch your rental property over a long haul—even though there is no rigid principle in this market. The choice to sell is altogether yours. There are a few exit procedures accessible to expand profits. Due to appreciation, you would probably sell your property at a more exorbitant price than you purchased it—which is the reason possessing a rental property is perhaps the best choice to make at this moment.

4.2 Profitable Rental Property – Features

Let us ponder over the prominent features you ought to consider while looking for the suitable rental property.

1. Neighborhood

The neighborhood wherein you purchase your rental property will decide the sorts of inhabitants you need to pull in and your vacancy rates. On the off chance that you purchase close to a college, the odds are that students would rule your pool of prospective occupants and you could struggle with the vacancies each summer. Know that a few towns attempt to debilitate rental changes by forcing over higher license charges and heaping on red tape.

2. A Worthwhile Property

A speculator should be persuaded that the given rental property is monetarily beneficial. Find out if the property in its current or improved state is truly worth spending your cash on. What amount of monthly lease inflows? Is it prone to generate for you? What is fixing and repairing costs? Is it justified, despite any trouble? These are the sort of inquiries you should perform before the investment. An ideal rental property ought to procure you a minimum yearly gross lease of 12% of the buying price. Apply the one percent rule to assist you with deciding about the rental type.

The monthly lease you would be gathering ought to, at any rate, be 1% of the house's estimation. This is perhaps a highly favorable feature of a rewarding rental property considered via prepared estate speculators. Furthermore, you could likewise include a monetary expert to assist you with deciding the cap rate. This will further assist you to determine whether the property is worthwhile.

3. Property Taxes

Such charges will differ broadly across your objective region, and you need to know about the amount you would be losing.

High property charges are not generally something adverse — in an incredible neighborhood that draws in long haul inhabitants, for instance, yet there are unappealing areas that likewise have high taxation.

The region's assessment office would have the complete tax data on a document, or you could converse with landlords in the network. Make certain to see whether property tax hikes are likely anytime soon. A financially troubled town might soar tax charges a long way past what a landowner could sensibly charge in lease.

4. Crime Rate

Nobody prefers to live in a high-crime neighborhood. The nearby police or public library ought to have precise crime rates insights for neighborhoods. Check the vandalism rates, and those for high and low-level crimes, and remember to note if a crime is on the ascent or decline. You might likewise need to get some information about the recurrence of police patrolling in your area.

5. Schools

Consider the standard of nearby schools in case you are managing family-sized homes. Even though you would be generally worried about monthly income, the general valuation of your rental property becomes a considerable factor when you, at last, sell it. On the off chance that there is nothing but sub-standard schools close by, your venture's estimation could be adversely impacted.

6. Job Market

Areas with greater employment prospects pull in more inhabitants. When you see a declaration about a significant organization moving into the territory, you could be certain that laborers looking for a spot to live in will rush there. This might render lodging costs to go up or down, contingent upon the sort of business included.

7. Future Development

The civil planning office would have data on plans and developments that have just been drafted into the region. When there is a great deal of development going on, it is likely to be a good development territory. Watch out for new advancements that could adversely impact the prices of encompassing properties. Extra new lodging could likewise be a rival to your property.

8. Amenities

Visit the area and look at the parks, eateries, recreational centers, cinemas, public transportation connections, and the wide range of various facilities that appeal leaseholders. City Hall might have promotional writings which could give you a thought of where the best mix of public comforts and private property could be found.

9. Average Rents

Rental inflows will make you a living, so you need to know the region's average lease rates. Ensure any property you consider could afford enough lease to cover your home loan installments, tax charges, and different costs. Examine the region thoroughly to anticipate where it might be going in the following five years. If you could manage the cost of the region presently however taxes are likely to expand, a moderate property today could imply bankruptcy later.

10. Number of Vacancies and Listings

If an area has an unexpectedly high number of postings, it might flag either an occasional cycle or a declining neighborhood — you would need to discover which one it is. In any case, high vacancies prompt landlords to bring down rents to allure inhabitants. Lower vacancy rates permit landowners to raise rent installments.

11. Adequate Sanitation

You could not discuss the characteristics of a gainful rental property without likewise discussing the sanitation facilities. There is a requirement that the rental property you plan to purchase be in a spot with sufficient sanitation. Inhabitants will, in general, avoid places with poor cleanliness and sanitation. The cleaner the house and the area are, the higher the measure of benefits you could make from it.

12. Territories Devoid of Natural Calamities

Another significant component of a progressive rental property is that it ought not to be situated in a territory inclined to natural catastrophes. With calamities and disasters, you truly cannot state if an area is resistant to obliteration. It is simply an issue of seeking after the best. Anyplace, there are regions which from past events have been known to be exceptionally inclined to cataclysmic events. These incorporate fiascos, for example, cyclones, typhoons, windstorms, fierce blazes, storms, and also earthquakes. In case of such calamities, one loses all his speculation. This could be very unfortunate if you additionally lacked an insurance cover against such outcomes.

13. Favorable Climate

Locality's climate also has a significant impact on the achievement of a productive rental property investment business. Houses situated in areas with harsh climates often battle to draw in customers. It is consequently essential that you pick an area with the ideal climate and atmosphere for your property. Follow and select the correct climatic zones, keep away from urban areas which would, in general, have a harsh and extreme climate. Likewise, stay away from territories which are inclined to floods and even flames.

All sources are significant to get data from; however, getting the information directly or from individuals who live there is abundantly valued. It is unequivocally endorsed that you should converse with occupants who lease the properties as they would speak the truth about living in the area and all the advantages and disadvantages therein. Stroll around the neighborhood during night and day times or on various days so you could have a genuine experience.

4.3 Purchasing First Rental Property – Tips and Tricks

The following tips might help those who are aiming to purchase their first rental investment property.

1. Could you be a Landlord?

If you are not good with handling everyday chores and looking after a property, plus do not have heaps of extra money, being a landowner might not be ideal for you.

2. Secure a Down-Payment

Rental properties, for the most part, require a bigger down-payment than do proprietor-occupied properties; they have more rigid approval prerequisites. The 3% you might have borne on the home where you presently live would not work for a rental property. You will require a minimum of 20% down-payment, provided that mortgage insurance is unavailable on rental properties. You might have the option to get the down-payment through bank financing, for example, personal borrowing.

3. Satisfy Personal Debt

Wise speculators might hold liability as an element of their portfolio venture strategy, yet the normal investors ought to avoid from it.

When you have unmanaged personal expenditures, buying a rental property might not be a rational move. Avoid setting yourself in an area where you come up short on the cash to make payments on your loan. Continuously create a line of safety.

4. Get the Right Location

Your least preferable choice would be owning a rental property in a territory that is declining instead of prospering. A city or district where the populace is developing and a rejuvenation plan are in progress speak to a potential venture opportunity. Location factor has been frequently discussed throughout this book.

5. Avoid High Financing Costs

The borrowing costs might be cheaper in 2020; however, the interest percentage on a rental property is higher than a conventional mortgage financing cost. If you choose to finance your buy, you will require a low mortgage installment that would not overly consume your monthly gains.

6. Buying or Financing?

Is it better to purchase with money or to finance your rental property? That relies upon your investing objectives. Paying money could help create positive monthly income. Take an investment property that costs $100,000 to purchase. With rental inflows, duties, depreciation, and income tax charge, the money purchaser could make $9,500 in yearly profit or a 9.5% yearly profit for the $100,000 speculation.

Then again, financing could grant you a higher return. For a financial specialist who ventures 20% on the house, with a 4% mortgage compounding, in the wake of taking out working costs and extra premium, the profit amounts to generally $5,580 every year. Income is lower for the speculator. However, a 27.9% yearly profit for the $20,000 venture is a lot higher than the 9.5% generated by the money purchaser.

7. Figure out Your Margins

Wall Street entities that purchase struggling properties rely on return rates of 5%-7% since, among different costs, they have to pay employees. Individuals should aim for a 10% return. Gauge administration expenses at 1% of the property valuation yearly.

8. Consider Unexpected Costs

Apart from the upkeep and maintenance costs, there might be other emergency expenditures, such as, rooftop harm from a storm, or burst pipes that decimate a kitchen floor. Plan to put aside 20% to 30% of your rental inflows for these kinds of expenses, so you have a reserve to pay for convenient fixes.

9. Ascertain Operating Expenses

Functional expenses on new property would be between 35% and 80% of your gross operational revenues. If you get $1,500 for rentals and your expenditures are $600 each month, you are at 40% for functioning expenses. For a much simpler count, follow the 50% rule. If you take $2,000 monthly lease, you would pay $1,000 in aggregate costs.

10. Considering Landlord Insurance

Secure your new venture: notwithstanding homeowners' insurance, think about buying landlord insurance. Such insurance usually covers lost rental revenues, property damage and loan protection — where an inhabitant or a guest endures injury because of property upkeep issues.

11. Dodge Fixer-Uppers

It is attractive to look for a bargained house and flip into a rental investment. If this is your initial property, that is likely to be an ill-conceived notion.

If you lack a contractual individual who performs quality work for less cost or you lack the home improvement skills, you probably would incur a great deal revamp. Search for a home that has been valued below the fair-market and requires minor fixes.

12. Decide Your Gains

Calculate your return for each contributed dollar. Stocks might give a 7.5% return, whereas securities might offer 4.5%. A pay off of 6% in your initial year as a landowner is assumed to be sound, since those digits should go up with time.

13. Be Aware of Your Legal Obligations

Rental proprietors should know the landowner-occupant laws in their region. It is critical to comprehend, for instance, your inhabitants' privileges and your commitments concerning security deposits, rent requirements, evacuation laws, fair lodging, and more to stay away from legitimate problems.

14. Purchase Low-Priced Houses

The costlier the house, the greater your ongoing costs would be. Various speculators suggest initializing with a $150,000 house in an emerging area. Also, specialists prompt never to get the most glamorous and worst houses available for purchase in the area.

15. Weigh Risks against the Rewards

In each monetary choice, you should decide whether the rewards outweigh the potential risks. Is rental properties investment sensible for you?

4.4 Buy Low and Rent High Strategies

The following buy low and rent high strategies applicable to rental properties might prove to be helpful for the novice real properties investors.

Step #1. Get Below Market-Value Property

One approach to "purchase low and lease high" is to get below-market price properties. This means, purchase those that are being offered for a price lower than the existing fair market value of such property. In any case, where would you be able to discover cheaper rental property available to be purchased? Here are a couple of venture property procedures to have them:

Short-Sale Properties

One of the speculation property procedures to purchase low and lease high is short deals. A short deal is a point at which the proprietor is behind on home-loan installments and is confronting foreclosure. Notwithstanding, they choose to assume control over issues and attempt to sell the property before the bank does.

The key here is that the dealer is persuaded enough to need to dispose the property sooner to bring in enough cash for covering the home-loan due. In this way, if they need to sell at a BMV (Below Market Value) price, they would escape foreclosure.

Foreclosed Properties

Another type of moderate speculation property strategy includes foreclosures. It is an identical notion to short-deals except that, in this situation, the bank has just assumed control over the selling cycle. So as opposed to managing the mortgage holder, you deal with the financial institution that financed that property initially. In such cases, the bank is likewise inspired to sell quickly. Along these lines, foreclosed houses available to be purchased are generally valued at whatever was outstanding in home-loan installments- often below market value.

Step #2. Do Your Due Diligence

After you have discovered a couple of potential speculation properties, it is the ideal opportunity for some math to be done. All speculation property methodologies need due perseverance and carrying out a venture property evaluation to ensure you discover one of the most productive speculations is crucial to your land speculation now.

Thus, before taking any further actions, check for yourself what the quantifiable profit for that investment property will be. This implies playing out a speculation property investigation to discover the ROI (Return on Investment).

Furthermore, research about why the dealer is selling the property for such a low price. For instance, was it a rental asset before being foreclosed? If so, for what reason did it not produce enough income to cover the home loan? These are the inquiries you need to carry out while applying these kinds of speculation property procedures.

Step #3. Remodel/Repair the Rental Property

Since you have learned how to purchase low, the time has come to confront reality with regards to these venture properties: as a rule, they are bothered properties. They are unlikely to be perfect structures. That is generally one reason behind why this kind of speculation property is so inexpensive.

Subsequently, you would have to repair the property. Regardless of whether it includes fixing the paints, replacing faucets or fixing a couple of lights around the house, it falls inside the remodeling class. Any progressions you apply to the rental property (except if they are unimportant) would prompt constrained appreciation. Fundamentally, it implies that your speculation property would consequently hike in worth. This would permit you to charge higher rentals, which leads us to our subsequent stage.

Step #4. Comparative Market Analysis (CMA)

Now, you are finished with the remodeling work, and your speculation property is prepared. You should then ask a question: "What amount would it be advisable for me to charge for lease?"

This is the point where the Comparative Market Analysis becomes an integral factor. The CMA helps a speculator set the valuing methodology for investment properties. The whole cycle depends on discovering "Real Estate Comparable". These are comparable investment properties that are in a similar area. This way, you could think about the rental cost and along these lines, ensure it is not very high or excessively low. While you lease at the market cost, you have been successful in purchasing low and lease high.

Step #5. Prepared to Rent Out

At last, you know the key to the purchase low lease high strategy that is extraordinarily compared to other venture property techniques. You have discovered cheapest properties, you dissected them for positive income, you have revamped them, and lastly, you need to set up your pricing technique. What is next? Lease it out. Get a decent marketing campaign for your investment property and stick to it. Get inhabitant applications and remember to do some occupant screening.

4.5 How to Start a Rental Property Business?

Purchase and-hold speculators, specifically, sustain to improve their long-term stance when they create a sound rental property investment plan. A verified rental property strategy could help design the frameworks and benchmarks which speculators need to acknowledge their accomplishment at a more significant level. Just one inquiry remains: what is an effective rental property plan?

If you are keen on beginning a rental property business, a few valuable lessons should be extracted from experience. The following takeaways might help build up an effective rental property investment plan, especially for the beginners.

Beginning a rental property venture is one matter, yet figuring out how to compose a rental property plan is something utterly different. While the two-sound comparable, the latter is more crucial that makes the previous one more sound. In any event, knowing how to begin a rental property business comes first. Consequently, investors should acclimate themselves with the fundamental steps first:

- Have a vision and compose the mission and vision statements.

- Set passive revenue and business objectives.

- Assemble a team framework that is helpful for progress.

- Gain an elevated-level viewpoint of the overall organization.

- Develop marketing frameworks and channels customized to a particular audience.

Figuring out how to begin a rental property venture does not vary much from other business endeavors. Investors merely need to realize a few key components before beginning; that way, they could begin their business on a strong foundation. Here are the absolute strides to be taken when drafting a rental property investment strategy and turning into an estate entrepreneur:

- Join a nearby REI (Real Estate Investment) club and begin networking.

- Select a niche and pick a rental property market.

- Sort out the best possible financing while securing it.

- Explore and recruit an estate manager.

- Adhere to the systems to enhance effectiveness.

- Deal with the properties and set the business at a manageable pace.

A genuinely incredible rental property strategy should underline one thing above everything else: the financial specialist's vision or mission. What a speculator would like to accomplish by putting resources into the estate might at the same time, fill in as inspiration and a guide when times are not exactly ideal. In this way, financial specialists should pause for a moment to consider why they are contributing. Knowing their "why" will help speculators work out a sound business technique; one that gets them closer to their objectives with every single venture. Thus, those without a mission would not know what course to head, which does not sound rational for any rental property business.

Purchasing a rental property is only the initial step on a passive revenue speculating excursion. Sooner or later, investors would need to sort out the ways to get tenants for generating inflows. As a general rule, financial specialists would depend on their property supervisors to fill vacancies. Should an investor fail to recruit a property manager, there are different approaches to discover occupants, some of which include:

- Social media

- Rental sites

- Print media or newspaper

- Neighborhood bulletin boards

- Neighborhood Realtors

- Informal marketing

- Past tenants

- Direct mail strategies

There might be no other prominent morale-booster than a rental property venture plan that works out as expected. By outlining your exact objectives—and the frameworks you would utilize to accomplish them—you would find wealth-generation targets more feasible than you ever expected.

4.6 Common Real Property Mistakes by the Beginners

These real estate errors are more frequent than you could imagine and should not become a barrier to your success.

1. Short-Term Expectations

Numerous first-time real properties investors purchase venture properties with the desire for gigantic returns in a very limited time. Regardless of whether you have put assets into a rental inflows property or are hoping for the property's value appreciation, tolerance should be your closest companion when receiving rewards from your real estate speculation.

2. Not Negotiating

Purchasers and sellers both have their particular incentives. Hence, effective bargains on offered prices could satisfy both the purchasers and sellers. Notwithstanding the price, you could negotiate the provisions of the deal and the obligations of the two parties.

3. Spending a Lot

Ensure that you are much educated on the most proficient method to discover the market price and that you have had a correct analysis. A property needs to have a high investment yield to legitimize its cost.

4. Not Knowing the Basics

Turning into a realtor need not require particular education, therefore eliminating entry barriers. However, numerous investors commit basic real estate errors since they lack the primary investment know-how that is essential for their advancement in the field.

5. Misinterpreting Cash Flows

New investors often miss a back-up plan and get caught off-guard when a vacancy is created. Landlords should, therefore, anticipate the adverse events around the corner and plan accordingly.

Chapter 5: Essential Tips for Real Estate Investment

Real property investment does not accompany a guide map, and the way to wealth is usually twisted. That being stated, there are strategies you could adopt to put yourself correctly and guarantee your best possibilities for progress. Tuning in to realtors and effective speculators is an ideal approach, to begin with.

1. Get your Homework Done Before Consulting the Paid Advisors

Generally, your trusted counselors (tax accountant, wealth manager and broker) might propose you to avoid real estate investment in your portfolio. They might, for the most part, give reasons that it is excessively management-intensive or illiquid. Those could be legitimate contentions depending on your particular circumstance, yet that is not the genuine explanation they need you to dodge real estate.

Stockbrokers do not get paid or commissioned for you to put resources into real estate unless they expect you to buy a non-exchanged, high-cost REIT (Real Estate Invest Trust), yet now you would know their actual incentive. You should perform your evaluation and analysis first to determine if the potential income from the real estate speculation is ideal for you.

2. Set your Timeline and Budget (and try following both)

You should put aside over 50 % of your spending plan as reserves, particularly as a new speculator. Your budget quite often exceeds more than anticipated, and while you are performing house-rehabbing, one issue could lead to another one.

For instance, fixing a mere pipe-leakage may transform into supplanting the pipe, eliminating damaged mold and restoring the drywall. Something very similar goes for the timeline; if your timetable is 60 days, the venture could rather take 90 days. With added costs, comes additional time.

3. Deal with Your Ventures Same as a Business

Real estate speculation is a business, and just like other businesses, it demands purposeful organization, management and execution. Efficient individuals govern the most effective businesses at each level of organization.

Those who disregard this reality might face multiple complications and hurdles. Notwithstanding how large or small-scaled you need to develop your real properties investment business, if you need to succeed, you should operate it as a business.

4. Discover Rental Investment Properties in Arising Neighborhoods

Rental property dealing is one of the most rational approaches to get engaged with real estate speculations. Arising neighborhoods offer tax incentives and development potential for investors. Purchasers that buy properties in arising neighborhoods expand their gains and assure that their revenues cover the expenses.

Then again, a definitive objective of estate speculation is to purchase a property in a promising location. At the point when you are ready to work on a neighborhood before it improves, you would encounter value appreciation to a great degree. You would likewise be ready to knock up rents fundamentally later on. The reason would be that the territory around your property will be improving and more affluent individuals will be moving into the region.

In case you can anticipate which territories will undergo the greatest future appreciation, you could without much of a stretch double your income in 2-3 years. Take regions like Columbia Heights in Washington D.C., Williamsburg in New York and The Arts District in Los Angeles. Had you put resources into any of these zones before they started to appreciate, you would have brought in twice your inflows in only a couple of brief years.

5. Avoid Over-leveraging Yourself

You could be effective for quite a while and yet go broken if each of your rental properties is highly mortgaged. When you keep a portion of your rentals clear and free while some of them financed, then you would have a decent blend of security while still stretching the resources. Do it the correct way, and several longer-than-anticipated vacancies or plunges in your income should not be your career-end.

6. Diversify your Ventures

There is a maxim that the leading real estate venture is the one that is in your back-yard. While there is legitimacy to understanding the territory in which you are contributing, you are in actual restricting your profit potential by merely thinking about a limited geographic region. By considering speculations in different cities and states, you would have huge access to potential speculations and eventually better chances for gains. Investment across a huge geographical region, likewise diversifies your speculations and secures your portfolio against the instability of neighborhood markets.

7. Purchase a Duplex

At your beginners' level, you would want to purchase a solitary family home or a duplex. Specialists propose going with a duplex.

Duplexes are commonly situated in moderate zones prepared for development. This makes them phenomenal speculation for a first-time real property's investor.

Different benefits of putting resources into duplexes include:

- Capacity to keep watch on your property day in and day out.

- Home-loan benefits when you purchase a duplex that you likewise live in.

- Duplexes enable speculators to house-hack. House hacking implies that a property owner could live inside one unit and lease the other, which has numerous advantages.

House Hacking

House hacking implies that you dwell in one unit and lease the nearby unit for income. With this strategy, you will live in your venture property while additionally watching out for it consistently. You would likewise presumably preclude troublesome inhabitants that make late payments and are noisy since they will realize they are living close to their landlord.

8. Secure Yourself with an LLC (Limited Liability Company) Investment

When putting resources into a property, you need to ensure to guard yourself against all the related risks. The ideal approach for this is to make a Limited Partnership or a Limited Liability Company, as opposed to putting resources into your name. Like this, if an occupant is injured and chooses to record a claim, such legal entities could secure your resources. At last, you would lose the cash you had contributed. Furthermore, having a limited company could secure your retirement fund if something adverse happens on your property.

9. Consider Recruiting a Property Supervisor

Consider employing a property controller, particularly when you plan on having properties in various areas. Property directors will administer the day-to-day activities of your venture property. Their basic role is to ensure that your property is kept up to the desired standards and that matters are going smoothly. For estate speculators purchasing properties outside of their neighborhood, property management is a need.

10. Increase the Value of Your Property

You can without much of a stretch improve the estimation of a property through some recovery work. This is known as value-addition. You do not need a development foundation or pay a huge sum to increase the value of a property. For instance, supplanting your rooftop costs around $3,000 and you could purchase new countertops for $30 per square feet. With such modest upgrades, you could considerably raise the worth of your property right away.

11. Avoid Investing in a REIT

Investing in a REIT resembles pooling resources into a stock. At the point you put resources into a REIT, you are providing a property speculation fund cash to purchase properties on your own. Placing resources into REITs used to be an extremely safe bet. Considering the ongoing poor health conditions, it is recommended to avoid REITs for an anticipated future. REITs are generally centered on business properties which have been altogether more influenced by COVID-19 than residential structures.

The ongoing pandemic and social-distancing would affect all business resources in various manners:

- **Multi-family:** People would need to keep a noteworthy distance from one another even after the relaxation of lockdown orders.

- **Offices:** Companies are at last beginning to acknowledge how simple and advantageous work-from-home approach is because facilities such as Zoom and Slack exist. This would keep them from needing to spend a heft of their financing on lease.

- **Retail:** Their demand would be affected for evident reasons.

Additionally, when you put resources into a REIT, you are not generally figuring out anything about real estate investment. An ideal approach to begin is to apply these tips and make a plunge.

12. Make a Network

Building a strong network with other real estate speculators could offer significant help and generate opportunities for both experienced and new estate speculators. It would help if you focused on establishing ties with more experienced speculators and even think about getting a mentor. Since a lot of real estate investments depend on experiential knowledge, experienced speculators comprehend the importance of forging effective ties and many people wish that they had begun significantly sooner.

13. Know the Standards and Guidelines

There are many guidelines that speculators reveal after being in the business for some time. For instance, you might be thinking about transforming a cellar into a second leasable unit. Much to your dismay, you discover that to be unlawful in the city your property is located in. It will help if you focus on zoning legislation, as they are in general contrast in every neighborhood market. For instance, you need to consider twice before transforming the primary floor of a structure you purchase into a co-working area since local division laws may disallow it.

You should not expect to include an additional room or second story to a structure; always go for the verification first. Regardless of whether you can acquire a permit, it will help if you comprehend the level of work needed to get a license before you begin with the process.

14. Produce Referrals

Wise speculators create a huge part of their business through references. Along these lines, it is vital that you establish your network and respectfully deal with other investors. This incorporates any colleagues, customers, inhabitants, and anybody with whom you have had an interaction before.

Real estate speculating groups are predominant, and severing one tie might conceivably prompt a lot more ties being cut-off. The best estate speculators give greater consideration to the details. They are likewise ordinarily open to criticism, including objections and concerns, and positively demonstrate their business. This permits speculators to erect the sort of notoriety that renders different real property speculators keen on collaborating with them later on and alluding their companions as well.

15. Hire an Accountant

Converse with any accomplished investor, and you would learn that taxes contain a critical segment of their yearly costs. Other than being costly, if you record your taxes inaccurately or miss an installment you should have made, the costs will be altogether higher. Understanding the existing tax laws could be exceptionally hard and time-consuming apart from the current business. This is particularly valid for speculators purchasing properties in several states, as the taxation laws could radically vary for each state. Savvy estate investors would quite often hold the services of a certified, trustworthy accountant to deal with their books. The accountant expenses are usually negligible when contrasted with the reserve funds they would generate for your business.

16. Follow a Plan

Real property investors should move towards their exercises as a business professional to build up and accomplish short-and-long-haul objectives. A business strategy is a smart thought to create, as it likewise permits financial specialists to envision the bigger perspective, which enables them to continue focusing on the significant objectives as opposed to any minor misfortunes.

Real estate investment could be demanding and complicated, and a strong arrangement could keep speculators coordinated and on the undertaking. The plan should incorporate assessed costs and inflows of money from rentals, the number of units to claim, when to repair or overhaul units, demographic modifications, and other matters that could affect your speculation over the long run.

17. Be Honest

Estate speculators are typically not committed to maintaining a specific promise of morals. Although it is anything but difficult to exploit this circumstance, successful investors keep up high moral guidelines. Since real estate speculating includes individuals, specialist's standing is probably going to be extensive. Viable real property investors realize it is smarter to be reasonable, instead of perceiving what they could pull off.

18. Know the Market

Successful estate speculators obtain a top to bottom information on their chosen markets, for example, narrowing in on a specific geographic district and zeroing in on private versus business properties.

Staying informed concerning the latest trends, involving any alterations in customers' spending behaviors, mortgage and unemployment rates, to give some examples, lets speculators recognize current conditions and plan for what is yet to come. This empowers them to anticipate when patterns might change, creating possible chances for the investor.

19. Set up a Niche

It is significant for speculators to build a concentration to pick up the profundity of information fundamental for success. Setting aside the effort to construct this degree of comprehension of a particular territory is essential for long haul achievement. When a specific market has been mastered, the speculator could proceed onward to additional zones utilizing a similar in-depth methodology. A few niches could be low-revenue multi-unit lodging, high-end residential or rustic farm zones.

20. Remain Educated

Likewise, with any business, it is essential to be updated with the laws, guidelines, patterns and terminologies that structure the premise of real property speculator's business. Speculators who fall behind might risk losing energy in their businesses as well as face lawful repercussions if laws are overlooked or broken. Effective speculators remain instructed and consistent with any administrative alterations or economic patterns. Also, remain updated with tax, real estate, and loaning laws and guidelines that could straightforwardly or by implication sway your business.

21. Comprehend the Risks

Securities exchange speculators are immersed with ordinary alerts concerning the innate dangers engaged with speculating and the potential for losses.

Real estate speculators, nonetheless, are more expected to come across the commercials asserting the exact inverse: that it is anything but difficult to generate inflows from real estate. Judicious investors comprehend the dangers—regarding real estate bargains as well as the lawful ramifications included—and make adjustments to their businesses to decrease those risks.

22. Retain All the Important Contacts

While you might have the authority, you are restricted in what you could do to the property yourself. Have a list of go-to individuals who should help you with your speculation. Property supervisors, a lawyer, a CPA, money lenders and realtors are exceptionally significant assets. Likewise, remember anybody who would keep your property well-maintained: electricians, plumbers, an inspector, a handyman, contractors and the pest controlling experts. While you might not need every one of these individuals forthright, it is rational to have a couple of dependable numbers to call.

23. Earn a Decent Name for Yourself

Your character, standing and identity lay on your monetary standing and experience. By monetary standing, we mean your monetary history, i.e., insolvency, credit score, and other aspects. Past monetary issues might debilitate some and consequently consider themselves unfit to enter the business. Notwithstanding, a great many people could strive to improve their records and push ahead.

Additionally, your experience and track record matter. They would be utilized to assess you against others in the field, and they characterize your identity and what you have achieved. Make a history for yourself that you would proudly share.

24. Create a Ground-Breaking Presentation that would Justify Itself

People prefer visuals. It would be the best if you make an informative and rousing presentation that portrays your organization's essence such that it is both aesthetically pleasing and productive. It ought to incorporate what your identity is, what you have accomplished and what you would offer. This progression is essential to the procedure as it merges everything referenced up until now and could be a make-or-break instant with regards to the potential investors.

25. Understand the Deal

If you are not much experienced or do not have a broad history, yet you possess a decent deal, speculators would come in any case. A decent arrangement is a sensible one, is priced rightly and could give a decent investment return. In case you have the right knowledge and tools, you are honest and, above all, your deal is rational, then you would have higher chances of attracting investors.

26. Honor your Responsibilities

This point should be complied with regardless of anything. Your trustworthiness as an individual is important. Property speculation business includes risks and demands mutual trust between all groups. Your statement is the most important thing you have to bring to the table.

27. Prioritize Funding

This measure is quite simple: for your venture to succeed, you need speculators. Before all else, a large degree of your speculators would probably be family and friends who are generous enough to help out. Inevitably, you might get a few companions of acquaintances to contribute through verbal exchange or basic marketing, and gradually, you would start to create your investors' network.

Likewise, as examined above, you need to encircle yourself with intelligent, honest and profoundly energetic and motivated people. Among these should be a lawyer, a bookkeeper, a few real estate agents and advertising professionals.

28. Comprehend the Economics and Get a Mentor

Real estate bargains that seem to be the most appealing and are least demanding to explore, for instance, joining a crowdfunding site, buying a property having a tenant and the executives set up, or getting associated with an open-market-traded estate speculation trust – generate the smallest returns. The highly rewarding chances are those which no one else considers about - the ones which you explore and create.

With a sound economy, higher consumer confidence, generally low stock volumes, and incredibly low borrowing costs comes an ideal time to flip houses. Sound economy and high customer confidence provide retail purchasers with an inclination that presently is a decent chance to buy instead of retreating in dread and continue leasing. Lower interest rates enable retail purchasers to invest in even more houses than if the charges were at traditional normal levels, such as 6 percent. Low inventory levels render bidding wars by retail buyers, which raises the selling-prices that speculators offer their flipped property for.

Thus, if you could discover the deals before the competition, you could convert a small amount of cash into a great deal in a slightly brief period by house flipping. In case you are looking for tax-relieved passive revenue, on account of the ascent of the sharing economy and facilitations like HomeAway and Airbnb, short-haul leasing of residential properties is creating the highest yields. (It is normal to acquire more than a 20 percent return on decent properties in visionary locations.)

Tragically, real estate is brimming with entanglements. Getting taught through respectable online sources could help; however, an article, book, or how-to video might be of little aid with responding to the main inquiries you would have at the peak of a deal. That is when an authentic real property mentor turns out to be an important asset.

29. Gauge the Kind of Return You Look Forward To

There are various ways that new investors could use to get returns from their estate ventures. Firstly, you could flip and fix the area, or you could put resources into a property and hold on for its worth to soar. Usually, be that as it may, what you are searching for is a rental return. This implies that you put resources into a private or business property and lease the spot. This way, you get a passive revenue for life that you could use for various things.

To the extent your benefit goes, you initially need to comprehend that business and private properties give varying returns. Business properties, for the most part, return 4 to 5 percent of their complete worth consistently, while private properties should restore 1 to 2 percent consistently. This is the purported one percent rule of rental land. Remember, however, that the expense of lease develops after some time, which implies that an existing projection is not the impression of what lies ahead.

30. Purchase Low

Real property investment could be contrasted with putting resources into a dividend-generating stock. The degree of profitability depends on how modest you purchased the product. Notwithstanding, you would need to take a gander at the profit for the speculation. An inexpensive little house in a hazardous area could be purchased for minimal expenditure. However, you would not get much cash from it.

31. Explore the Hidden Markets

The ideal approach is purchasing a property from a troubled seller since you could get it at a cost much lower than the fair market price. Disregard foreclosed auctions; this could yield bargains, yet you would frequently discover properties in critical need of a fix. Rather, search for homes with struggling dealers who have not still placed the property on the market. The couple experiencing a separation or family that needs to sell mother's home after her passing away are the ideal dealers; they need to get the cash, and the purchaser is presumably getting an all-around looked-after home.

32. Think about Non-Traditional Real Property Investments

Realize that real property investment does not need to rise to a decision between putting resources into single-family homes and high rises. You could put resources into places of business, stockpiling unit buildings, modern spaces, and warehouses. These produce rental inflows. On account of workplaces and industrial structures, you might have the option to lessen general costs through a triple-net rent where the inhabitant covers fundamental insurance and bears the maintenance and property taxes. Your venture at that point yields consistent income with not many cash-based costs.

33. Obtain a Landlord Policy

A landowner strategy is a protection strategy that could secure you all through your term as a speculation property owner or property chief. Get a quote for a property management strategy before getting the deal done. By getting a real insurance strategy or a quote ahead of time, you could precisely set monthly costs and set the lease at a value that would deliver positive income.

34. Request an Appraisal

Property evaluations are amazingly useful because they dissect the past, current, and anticipated future estimation of the speculation property. Without a property examination, you are left unsure what the structure is worth. An examination will likewise give a decent indication of the installment to charge in the monthly lease for the property.

35. Visit the Property at Whatever Point Possible

It would be to your substantial advantage to visit the property on numerous occasions before making a buy. Make sure to see the property at various times and days of the week.

For instance, if the nearby walking band arbitrarily rehearses on your road at 7 pm on a Thursday, at that point, you would need to think about it. Or on the other hand, you may find that the night traffic makes a parking garage in your front yard, as individuals take alternate routes attempting to return home. All in all, while Google Maps is a useful instrument, nothing beats visiting the property yourself.

36. A few Questions to Clarify Your Investment Goals

The accompanying inquiries would help precisely limit your objectives, set sensible goals, and keep you on target to settle on the correct land venture decisions.

- When do you intend to resign?
- When you resign, what amount of cash will you need to cover your bills?
- What are your present retirement pay sources?
- What amount of cash would you put into the estates?
- Would you like to secure the property for future development, or do you need income today?
- Do you have a reasonable credit?

- Do you have to plan for school, travel, or your parent's long-haul care?

- Are you searching for a tax reduction?

After responding to these inquiries, ensure you set a period for every one of your objectives and do all that is conceivable to adhere to such a timeline.

Real estate speculation signifies a phenomenal opportunity to investigate new monetary avenues, broaden your portfolio, and prepare ahead for your retirement (or other monetary objectives). By following the above real estate venture tips, you could begin an effective real estate speculation journey.

Conclusion

During the era of the current poor health condition and wavering economies, people want to move towards an option that provides a continuous stream of revenues. Real estate investment has come as a ray of hope under such circumstances. Among various classes, rental investment properties stand for being a passive source of positive cash flows. Rental properties not only allow persistent income streams but other incentives as well, including the tax leverages, gains from property value appreciation and a hedge against inflation.

This guide book covers an extensive area for the strategies investors could use for buying low and renting high. Step by step guide has been provided for those stepping into the real estate market. Drafting a detailed business plan, for instance, would be the first step to starting an experience in rental property markets. Creation of a sound network for a morale boost and successful handling of everyday operations, calculating the potential returns, setting up margins and deciding a secure source of finance count a lot when it comes to structuring wise investment strategies.

The location should be a key consideration for rental investment properties. Also, one question which the prospective investors should raise is whether they are ready to be landlords. The most successful landlords have the required time and capital, along with property management and people-handling skills. Consistency, determination and patience are demanded for an effective real estate investment.

This comprehensive guide has been aimed at educating the beginners about the real properties investment know-how and likewise help them discover ultimate strategies to get the best returns. We hope the best for readers in their real estate journey.

www.ingramcontent.com/pod-product-compliance
Lightning Source LLC
Chambersburg PA
CBHW071719210326
41597CB00017B/2535